CRACKING LABOUR'S GLASS CEILING

TRANSFORMING LIVES THROUGH WOMEN'S UNION EDUCATION

CINDY HANSON, ADRIANE PAAVO
AND SISTERS IN LABOUR EDUCATION

FOREWORD BY BARBARA BYERS

FERNWOOD PUBLISHING • HALIFAX & WINNIPEG

Cover graphic with permission of carol weaver and the Prairie School for Union Women. The
graphic is symbolic of women's lives: Bread, roses and solidarity

Editing: Brenda Conroy
Cover design: John van der Woude
Printed and bound in Canada

Published in Canada by Fernwood Publishing
32 Oceanvista Lane, Black Point, Nova Scotia, B0J 1B0
and 748 Broadway Avenue, Winnipeg, Manitoba, R3G 0X3
www.fernwoodpublishing.ca

Fernwood Publishing Company Limited gratefully acknowledges the financial support of the
Government of Canada, the Manitoba Department of Culture, Heritage and Tourism under the
Manitoba Publishers Marketing Assistance Program and the Province of Manitoba, through the
Book Publishing Tax Credit, for our publishing program. We are pleased to work in partnership
with the Province of Nova Scotia to develop and promote our creative industries for the benefit
of all Nova Scotians. We acknowledge the support of the Canada Council for the Arts, which last
year invested $153 million to bring the arts to Canadians throughout the country.

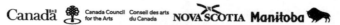

Library and Archives Canada Cataloguing in Publication

Title: Cracking labour's glass ceiling transforming : lives through women's union education / by
Cindy Hanson, Adriane Paavo and Sisters in Labour Education.
Names: Hanson, Cindy, 1961- author. | Paavo, Adriane, 1963- author. | Sisters in Labour
Education,
author.
Description: Includes bibliographical references.
Identifiers: Canadiana (print) 20190063149 | Canadiana (ebook) 20190063661 | ISBN
9781773632094
(softcover) | ISBN 9781773632100 (EPUB) | ISBN 9781773632117 (Kindle)
Subjects: LCSH: Labor unions—Study and teaching. | LCSH: Women labor union members—
Education.
Classification: LCC HD6483 .H36 2019 | DDC 331.87071—dc23

CONTENTS

Labour in Canada Series

This volume is part of the Labour in Canada Series, which focuses on assessing how global and national political economic changes have affected Canada's labour movement and labour force as well as how working people have responded. The series offers a unique Canadian perspective to parallel international debates on work and labour in the United States, Great Britain and Western Europe.

Authors seek to understand the impact of governments and markets on working people. They examine the role of governments in shaping economic restructuring and the loss of unionized jobs, as well as how governments promote the growth of low-wage work. They also analyze the impacts of economic globalization on women, minorities and immigrants.

Contributors provide insight on how unions have responded to global labour market deregulation and globalization. They present accessible new research on how Canadian unions function in both the private and public sectors, how they organize and how their political strategies work. The books document recent success stories (and failures) of union renewal and explore the new opportunities emerging as the labour movement attempts to rebuild the economy on sound environmental principles.

Over the past thirty years, the union movement has increasingly been put on the defensive as its traditional tactics of economic and political engagement have failed to protect wages, maintain membership and advance progressive agendas. Yet there has been far too little discussion of how the terrain of Canadian politics has shifted and how this has, in turn, affected the Canadian labour movement. There has also been far too little acknowledgment of working people's attempts to develop new strategies to regain political and economic influence. This series aims to fill these major gaps in public debate.

The volumes are resources that can help unions successfully confront new dilemmas. They also serve to promote discussion and support labour education programs within unions and postsecondary education programs. It is our hope that the series informs debate on the policies and institutions that Canadians need to improve jobs, create better workplaces and build a more egalitarian society.

Series editors
Stephanie Ross and Larry Savage

Acronyms

AFL-CIO	American Federation of Labor and Congress of Industrial Organizations, the United States workers' central
CAW	Canadian Auto Workers (now Unifor)
CLC	Canadian Labour Congress
CLUW	Coalition of Labor Union Women
CNA	Canadian Nurses Association
CUPE	Canadian Union of Public Employees
CUPW	Canadian Union of Postal Workers
CUT	Central Unitaria de Trabajadores, the Colombian workers' central
ETFO	Elementary Teachers' Federation of Ontario
EWS	Equity and Women's Services
FLOC	Farm Labor Organizing Committee
FNMI	First Nations, Métis, Inuit
FWTAO	Federation of Women Teachers' Associations of Ontario
IAM	International Association of Machinists and Aerospace Workers
IBT	International Brotherhood of Teamsters
IFF	intersectional feminist frameworks
LGBTQ	Lesbian, Gay, Bisexual, Transgender, Queer
L4T	Leaders for Tomorrow, a women's leadership education program developed by ETFO
Mass AFL-CIO	Massachusetts state body of the AFL-CIO
MassCOSH	Massachusetts Coalition for Occupational Safety and Health
MEC	Movement of Women Workers and Unemployed Women: "Maria Elena Cuadra" in Nicaragua
OPSEU	Ontario Public Service Employees Union
OPSTF	Ontario Public School Teachers' Federation
PSAC	Public Service Alliance of Canada
PSI	Public Service International
PSUW	Prairie School for Union Women
SEIU	Service Employees International Union
SFL	Saskatchewan Federation of Labour
UALE	United Association for Labor Education (successor organization to UCLEA)
UCLEA	University and College Labor Education Association
UE	United Electrical, Radio and Machine Workers of America
USW	United Steelworkers
TED	(Technology, Entertainment, Design) Talk
WILD	Women's Institute for Leadership Development
WOAH	Women of African Heritage
WBB	Women Breaking Barriers, a women's leadership education program developed by CUPE

ACKNOWLEDGEMENTS

We are deeply grateful to the women who contributed to the chapters of this book for sharing their important work. We thank and acknowledge the Saskatchewan Federation of Labour, the Canadian Labour Congress and Canadian Union of Public Employees (National) for financial support in the preparation of this publication; the Faculty of Education at the University of Regina for funding the first study about the Prairie School of Union Women (PSUW); and the United Association for Labor Education for funding the second research study about the PSUW. And we thank Fernwood Publishing for supporting work on the theme of women-only labour education.

Last, but not least, we offer our gratitude and admiration to all the women who organize workshops and schools which offer their sisters the inspiration, support and tactics to stand up, speak out and lead.

LABOUR EDUCATION SCHOOLS FOR WOMEN ONLY

I welcome this book about women's leadership and labour education. It challenges all of us to work differently. For me, the story about the Prairie School for Union Women is central. The Prairie School for Union Women was born in Saskatchewan, Canada, at a time when there were few initiatives to promote women's leadership in unions. In the mid-1990s, we organized occasional women's conferences, but these were stand-alone events, not deliberately building toward anything.

Then, feminist and labour educator Sharon Hurd and I had a conversation after her return from the Pacific Women's Institute, a women-only school organized by union women in British Columbia and the north-western US. As I recall, Sharon asked, "Why can't we do something like this in Saskatchewan? Why can't we put on a school for women only?" So, in late 1994 or early 1995, we invited a group of Saskatchewan union women together who were interested in feminist education. The idea caught on, and the PSUW was created as a feminist-focused event that would view leadership development as a multifaceted, ongoing process, rather than as a single course a woman would take once.

We chose not to institutionalize the school inside the Saskatchewan Federation of Labour, although I was an active participant *and* the SFL president. This was one of the school's biggest strengths because it allowed women to organize it even if they could not get their union's official approval to participate. We used every stage of school planning to promote leadership. On the steering committee, women got to learn how to organize the logistics of a major event or learn about popular education. For me, the question always was: how are we providing opportunities for women to learn outside of the classroom itself?

I attended every school from 1996 until I moved on to the Canadian Labour Congress in 2002. I chose not to play the role of a labour diplomat at the school, but instead joined in the hands-on work of running the event because I needed to learn from the women who attended. I could not do that if I came across as the "official." When I was unpacking boxes along with every other volunteer or running errands for facilitators, participants felt more comfortable talking to me about what they wanted to see the school become or how they wanted to contribute. And it was a way of showing that leadership is not just a title, but that sometimes leaders give speeches and sometimes they pick up garbage. The school also became a place where I got re-energized by hearing about women's struggles in their workplace, communities and homes and about their ideas for what the labour movement needed to do in all these places to make change.

I welcome this book because I want women activists and labour educators to embrace the challenge to do this work differently — that is, not to look at leadership education as institutional. And not to think that there is only one way to "do" a women-only school. This book explores several rich examples, all of them with their strengths and successes. Look at these experiences, be inspired by them and then come up with your own ideas for a women-only school that meets your needs.

Now that I have retired from official positions in the labour movement, I have hopes as well as fears for the future of women-only education. I feel fear when I keep hearing people ask, "Do women really need these spaces anymore?" Well, yes, we do, and we are going to need them for a long time to come. We do not have equality yet. Our work of advancing women's leadership in this movement is not going to be completed quickly.

And I have hope that women-only schools will continue in a variety of forms, whether through individual unions or the CLC or federations or labour councils. Without women-only schools, where else do we provide spaces for women to discuss their status and role inside their unions and about how their leadership will be acknowledged? At this point, it is easier to be a woman leader, but it is not easy enough.

To the organizers of women-only labour schools, I say: be prepared to shake things up. Do not get stuck in a rut, especially when it comes to increasing the diversity of the women who attend. We need to be more disciplined and deliberate about increasing the participation of women from many backgrounds, orientations, abilities, ages and length of involvement with their union.

The energy that comes from women-only schools is the energy of taking risks on difficult topics, on difficult leadership issues and on providing the space for women to find the ways forward.

— Barbara Byers

UNION WOMEN'S LEARNING

Cindy Hanson and Adriane Paavo

Among the small but growing list of books and articles about adult learning inside the labour movement, too few look at union women's learning. Yet the health and viability of the trade union movement may rest on its ability to include women in membership and leadership, as well as to incorporate feminist values into its structures and processes (Briskin 2006; Briskin and McDermott 1993; Hanson 2015; Kirton 2017; Paavo 2006; Twarog, Sherer, O'Farrell and Coney 2016). Within the labour movement, feminists and other women activists see union education as a way to achieve gender-equality goals within unions and in the wider society. Women's labour education is one of the tools to "crack labour's glass ceiling" (Elkiss 1994: 25–42), and the chapters in this book describe some of the ways that tool has been used to make room for more women in all of our diversity.

One of the most significant experiments with feminist labour education in recent years is the Prairie School for Union Women (PSUW). Since 1997, women in unions affiliated with the Saskatchewan Federation of Labour have organized the annual school. Not only do participants attribute it with igniting their activism and recharging their batteries, but facilitators and union educators value it as a site where innovative practices and courses are welcome.

This book's authors have long and different connections to the Prairie School for Union Women — Adriane as one of its founders and a long-time organizer and facilitator; Cindy as collaborator in two important research projects about the school. Both are Saskatchewan-born feminists who work in adult education — Cindy in postsecondary education and Adriane inside the labour movement.

The Prairie School for Union Women brought Adriane and Cindy together and inspired this book. In the first place, the results of the two research studies into the school were worth sharing. But then union activists, many of whom had attended the PSUW, kept asking whether there would be a book about the school. And finally, the authors understood that the

PSUW does not stand alone but is part of a vibrant — if underappreciated — modern tradition of women-only labour education events, within individual unions and across union federations, in Canada, the United States and beyond.

All of the women-only education programs and methods described in this book are solidly rooted in trade unions. In other words, unions have either initiated and carried them out or else officially endorsed them. This distinction is useful to make because university-based labour educators have developed some of the programs described in these pages. But Adriane and Cindy were adamant that this book could not just be for academic purposes, although they hope that it will interest those who study unions and adult learning. This is a book for the women, men and others who engage in union learning as learners, activists, peer facilitators and those who work for unions and other social-justice organizations.

Not surprisingly, several chapters of the book analyze aspects of the Prairie School for Union Women. But no matter which women-only union learning program in Canada and the United States is examined, all chapters identify the methods attempted in pursuit of learner empowerment and transformation and assess how successful the outcomes were. The authors speak from firsthand experience: they were all involved in the development, implementation, research, facilitation and/or evaluation of the education programs, and all programs (schools and courses) continue to this day. Many of the authors have formal academic credentials, but for the most part they speak as practitioners in day-to-day adult-learning environments.

The first chapter, by Adriane Paavo and Barb Thomas, discusses course facilitation at the Prairie School for Union Women. Adriane and Barb have both designed and led facilitation-training courses at the school, and their passion and hopes for the school are evident in the chapter. They describe and assess the measures taken by the Prairie School for Union Women to develop women's leadership as facilitators (i.e., deliberately trained instructors) of union learning, the way feminism guides its practices and how attention to such details ensures the continuity of the school.

In Chapter 2, Cindy Hanson joins Adriane to describe two community-based participatory action research projects they initiated with the Prairie School for Union Women's Steering Committee. The first project explored how well the school was meeting its goals of developing women's personal and leadership skills, building solidarity among women workers and increasing knowledge about the labour movement. The stories expressed by study participants indicated that, in addition to meeting the goals of the school, the women experienced transformation in personal perspectives and in confidence building. The second study, carried out with funding from the United Association for Labor Education, identified which PSUW methods and structures contributed to transformation in learners and how that transformation might be sustained.

Chapter 3 explores the voices of Indigenous women who facilitated the course Union Women on Turtle Island. Cindy conducts an interview with Sandra Ahenekew and Yvonne Hotzak, who describe how they became involved in labour education and how they use the course to build knowledge about Indigenous women. Sandra and Yvonne share examples of storytelling and popular education methodologies from their facilitation practice.

In Chapter 4 Donna Smith takes a reflective stance on her work in labour education as a lesbian woman. She explains the history of lesbian, gay, bisexual, transgender and queer activism in the labour movement and how it affected labour education.

Chapter 5 is a retrospective on The Wall methodology by Bev Burke and Suzanne Doerge, long-time social-movement educators who created the methodology to empower women to take action on gender-based economic inequality. After two decades of facilitating The Wall with women in unions around the globe and in allied social-justice organizations, they reflect on the challenges, successes and applications of this visual and participatory methodology.

In Chapter 6 Helena Worthen, now a retired professor from the University of Illinois Labor Education Program, discusses the Regina V. Polk Women's Labor Leadership Conference, which she designed and ran for years. She offers a reflection of the impact of a "curriculum for women who needed to fight" inequality at home, work and in the union.

In Chapter 7, Dale Melcher, Tess Ewing and Susan Winning, labour educators based at the University of Massachusetts, examine best practices and challenges of the Women's Institute for Leadership Development and discuss it as a model of an effective and sustainable leadership development program for women in unions.

Chapter 8, by Carol Zavitz, with staff in the Equality and Women's Services department of the Elementary Teachers' Federation of Ontario, describes the structure and analyzes the impact of the union's Leaders for Tomorrow education program for women, as a means to increasing women's participation in union leadership.

In Chapter 9, Morna Ballantyne and Jane Stinson, retired national staff with the Canadian Union of Public Employees, discuss Women Breaking Barriers, the leadership program for women activists which they developed. Based on interviews with the program's first-year cohort, they evaluate the successes and challenges of the program in increasing women's sustained movement into union leadership.

Cindy and Adriane conclude the book with a Critical Love Letter about women's labour education in general and specific points about the PSUW.

They take a feminist view of the historical and conceptual roots of women's labour education in its contemporary form, all the while asking, is this what was intended? Are there things that we could be doing differently? What lessons can be learned from the record of existing schools? Taking such a critical view was, for the co-authors, part of putting theory into action — the praxis that Paulo Freire (2000) advocated and that should not be ignored in the practice of popular and political education.

There is no doubt that this collection is just a beginning. The authors hope it will inspire active dialogue about and development of new and exciting programs and methodologies. While each of us is justly proud of the program we created or worked with, all contributors to this book wish to see creative variation rather than rote imitation. Organized labour and social-justice organizations (in Canada, in the United States and globally) continue to buzz with learning activities. This book hopes it can be of interest and use to educators seeking to build more inclusive, vibrant movements.

CHAPTER ONE

FACILITATION TRAINING FOR UNION WOMEN

The Saskatchewan Experience

Adriane Paavo and Barb Thomas

From the first days of the Prairie School for Union Women (PSUW), we saw the school as an incubator for women's leadership. Designing and facilitating courses was an underdeveloped form of leadership that the annual intensive four-day school could address. We both played roles in creating the school's approach to facilitation and in helping to maintain and improve that approach over more than fifteen years.

To write this chapter, we asked: What did we do, as individuals and as part of the collective group of school organizers? Why was any of it significant? And what have we learned that might be useful for future women labour educators?

THE PSUW VISION

The PSUW had a vision: put popular education at the heart of the school from the beginning.[1] From the first planning meetings, held in the basement of the Regina Union Centre in 1995–96, the women who would midwife the birth of the PSUW were clear: all courses would use popular education principles and methods, for a few reasons. First, popular education invited contributions from all participants, who would learn from each other as well as from the facilitator. Second, this process of learning from each other built community and a collective sense of possibility. Third, popular education uncovers and invites analysis of power relations in order to change them. This is the heart of building a union movement with capacity to work for social justice.

Equally clear in the PSUW vision was that women would design and facilitate all courses, working in pairs, as co-facilitators. Popular education facilitation requires preparation, sharing power, listening and learning from those with less power, building collective agency and balancing task with care of people. These are all leadership skills the school promoted, whether we were conscious of it or not at the beginning.

By the mid-1990s, popular education had gained substantial legitimacy within the Canadian labour movement. But Saskatchewan, as well as other places, lacked a large pool of members, activists and staff with hands-on experience in using it to design and facilitate union learning. PSUW organizers could not just issue orders to "use popular education." Moreover, most established labour educators were men. In order to implement the PSUW vision, innovative women labour educators needed to create new practices and structures related to course design and facilitation.

FOCUS ON FACILITATOR PREPARATION

PSUW organizers proposed a new practice: offer facilitator preparation weekends each winter, to examine principles and techniques of popular education through practical activities. Preparation weekends were scheduled well in advance of each school and were officially sponsored by the Saskatchewan Federation of Labour (SFL). Facilitators at each upcoming school — and at other SFL schools and events — were strongly encouraged to attend, along

---

Example of a Facilitator Preparation Weekend

Each year, PSUW organizers asked that the weekend focus on a different key issue in effective labour education. One of the years when Barb Thomas co-facilitated the weekend, the focus was integrating equity into all aspects of union education. Day one linked harassment to wider structures of injustice. Participants developed some collective guidelines for recognizing and dealing with inequities in union education courses.

On day two, participants reflected on the practice of popular education. Barb challenged the notion that technical courses can't be taught using popular education, and she supported participants as they developed popular education activities that effectively explored "technical information." Together, the group analyzed the ways that power shapes how "technical" and "not technical" are defined, and by whom. Facilitation teams also worked on their courses, integrating what they learned into their designs. The evening focused on dealing with facilitation challenges in the moment, as they happened.

While these preparation weekends were well attended for the first ten or twelve years, by 2009, fewer facilitators signed up to come. The last one, to date, was held in 2011. School organizers attributed this to the facilitators' busy lives: it is hard to give up another weekend. Low attendance could also be a result of a growing familiarity with popular education and little turn-over in facilitators. Those asked to teach the same courses year after year feel less need to prepare. (See our later discussion of the "three years and rest" rule.) For whatever mixture of reasons, school organizers grew less insistent that facilitators attend the preparation weekends, and this weaker official backing has reduced their significance.

---

with their co-facilitator. Besides learning new theory and techniques, facilitators could practise troublesome segments of their course in "design clinics" and receive feedback and suggestions for change.

We were two of the labour educators asked to lead preparation weekends over the years. We saw how the weekends brought new facilitators of women's courses together with facilitators from more traditional union schools. These sessions consciously sought to strengthen a community of Saskatchewan union educators through sharing and trying out new practices together. Educators could then integrate these practices into the courses they were facilitating. Skeptics, who taught in more traditional, instructor-centred ways, were treated with respect at these events and encouraged to raise questions and engage in discussions about the merits of different pedagogical approaches.

Facilitator preparation weekends served not only to implement a consistent use of popular education methodologies, but also to communicate the importance of preparation. With their official labour-federation sponsorship, these weekends sent a message: "These courses are important, and they require your time and attention. Co-facilitators must work from a shared design and vision of their course."

CREATE STRUCTURES TO KEEP CHANGE HAPPENING

Another way that school organizers created deliberate practices and structures to implement the PSUW education vision was by establishing a program sub-committee to propose each year's list of courses and facilitators. Since any woman trade unionist could volunteer on a PSUW committee, the program sub-committee had the potential to be a democratic and innovative body.

There were other advantages to having recent school participants and facilitators create the school program. These women brought a passion for the school to their work. They could apply what they had learned about good union education to the organization of future schools, for the benefit of future participants. And the sub-committee became another place for women to practise leadership.

The program sub-committee made efforts to select "graduates" of the PSUW's popular education courses to be future facilitators. This was a good start inside the school itself, but there was no equivalent effort to help graduates gain recognition within their individual unions, which would have allowed them to use their new skills more frequently. When such communication happened, it was informal and accidental. For example, in the 2004 facilitation-skills course, Barb noticed that a participant from Adriane's union was showing promise. Barb made a point of talking to Adriane, who was able to involve the woman as a facilitator back in her home union. None of this would have happened, however, if Barb had not taken the initiative.

Three Years and Rest

The PSUW program sub-committee noticed how easy it was to avoid the hard work of identifying and supporting new facilitators, by sticking with "tried and trusted" veteran women. Consequently, it created a "three years and rest" rule. This meant that no individual facilitator (and in some cases, no individual course) would be on the schedule more than three years in a row. No matter how talented the facilitator was, she had to take a year off from facilitating at the school, so that someone else would have a chance to gain experience and the notice of others.

Strict adherence to the "three years and rest" rule started to erode in the mid-2000s. In fairness to school organizers, constantly recruiting new facilitators was labour-intensive. And the work of organizing the school was shifting from volunteers on the school steering committee to SFL staff. At the time of this writing, it is not unusual to have school facilitators well past their third consecutive year of facilitating. As noted earlier, it is likely that this has contributed to declining participation in the facilitator preparation weekends.

CREATE MORE FACILITATORS AND USE THEM IN MORE WAYS

The most elaborate new practice was to see PSUW participants as a pool of potential future designers and facilitators and to use the school itself to support the development of more skilled women educators. So organizers put a popular education design and facilitation course on the school curriculum and kept it there. Other courses rotated off and on the agenda, but "pop ed" has been offered every year since the first school in 1997, attracting sixteen to twenty participants each time. (It was offered but cancelled, for the first time ever, in 2015 due to low enrolment.)

Organizers hoped that women who took this course would be ready to facilitate at the school itself, but by the year 2000, we realized this was not happening. While women were enthusiastically taking the two-day popular education design and facilitation course, few felt ready to be in-the-classroom facilitators. School organizers responded by increasing the course time to four days, which was also part of a move to four-day courses throughout the school curriculum. The extra two days allowed participants to explore the basics of popular education, design an activity using popular education tools, co-facilitate and get feedback, and practise dealing with "scary" moments in facilitation. There was more time to build a community of women who could facilitate union education and who could support each other after the school. By 2005, this course was co-facilitated by an experienced popular educator and an emerging popular educator who was hoping to gain more experience. Although this pairing of facilitators was one way to introduce mentoring within the school, it remained informal. It depended on the experienced educator being willing to work a bit harder in the short term, and, in the long term, step aside in favour of their apprentice. School organizers did not explicitly request this of experienced facilitators, and the practice of mentoring within facilitation pairs was not widespread.

By 2006, school organizers realized that we needed to do more to create a larger cohort of female union educators. We had been framing "facilitation" narrowly, as a form of leadership that took place only in a classroom, when in fact there are many venues for facilitation, such as meetings and gatherings over a lunch-room table. Perhaps once women became comfortable with their abilities to educate in informal settings, they could more easily see themselves facilitating a course at a union school.

School organizers commissioned Barb to design Facilitation Skills for Everyday Union Work, also known as Popular Education Level One. This course was different from previous ones in that it provided participants with more opportunities to examine how good facilitation could make a difference in moments of interaction and learning in their unions. On day one, participants located themselves in their unions and diverse communities, and explored ways to open conversations, meetings and gatherings. During day one, women activists looked at their experiences in relation to racist and sexist behaviours, male-dominated meetings and resistance to conversation about equity, and how they might turn these experiences into opportunities for problem-solving.

On day two, women designed an activity for a meeting, gathering or other union event using popular education tools. They examined how design can either exclude or include people who are often marginalized in such events. During day three, women co-facilitated the event they planned and received feedback. Day four focused on creative ways to energize, change groupings of participants, ask good questions at different moments in an event and create conditions for action. Although action is the stated goal of many union events, it often fails to materialize if facilitators do not understand that people first need to feel a sense of belonging and confidence.

The existing course on classroom design and facilitation became Popular Education Level Two, which requires Popular Education Level One as a prerequisite. The courses are offered in alternating years to make it easier for women to follow the progression, and many did. However, it still did not seem to make the difference school organizers hoped for. Clearly, simply taking a course on facilitation — no matter how good the course — was not sufficient to give women all the confidence, skills and insights to move into the role of a classroom facilitator.

MENTOR MORE DELIBERATELY AND FORMALLY

Around 2006, we began to experiment with ways to mentor emerging facilitators at the school. Women who had already taken Levels One and Two could sign up as apprentices in a mentoring program. In our first experiment, we brought the apprentices together during lunch breaks to discuss the facilitation techniques they had observed in their courses that day. Apprentices were given assignments, such as observing how facilitators handled any conflict situations in the classroom, and reported back for further discussion.

By 2013, PSUW organizers decided to try a second, more intensive experiment and created Popular Education Level Three as a new, stand-alone class. Adriane coordinated the mentoring program in that first year, recruiting women who had completed Levels One and Two and engaging them in four full days of supported practice. Apprentices started by reviewing the spiral model and other popular education design basics, but spent the bulk of their time on two assignments. The first was to design a short module for use during one of the school's morning plenaries or closing session. The second assignment was to facilitate a portion of one of the courses running at that week's school. For both assignments, apprentices helped one another prepare, observed one another in action and provided feedback.

The results of this mentorship model, coordinated a second time in 2014 by Judy Shannon, appeared promising. The three 2013 participants were quickly recruited to facilitate at the Saskatchewan Federation of Labour's health and safety conference and at the 2014 PSUW. Four women participated in the mentoring program in the following year. While two were from out of province and one had to decline an invitation to facilitate for family reasons, the other co-facilitated at two federation events since taking the training. 2014 was the last mentoring program to date.

WHY DOES ATTENTION TO FACILITATION MATTER?

More Women Start Facilitating

The emphasis on training women in popular education facilitation created a noticeable shift in the gender of union facilitators in Saskatchewan. It has become easier to think of qualified women to facilitate the SFL's co-ed week-long labour school using practices and principles of popular education and increasingly harder to think of men who could do so. This started happening within three or four years of the launch of the PSUW in 1997. school organizers estimated that at least a hundred women have taken some combination of Popular Education Level One, Two and Three courses over the life of the school.

Contributes to Participants' Personal Transformation

Recent PSUW research (cited and described in Chapter 2) shows how popular education contributes to transformation. Research participants, who had attended one or more schools, described how the courses created opportunities for them to tell their own stories, which in turn provided solutions and strategies for other women. Facilitators were described as being role models and examples to other women wanting to take action. Additionally, deliberate design and facilitation choices created welcoming and inclusive classroom environments where sharing and confidence flourished. A quote from one of the participants spoke to the increased confidence:

> They [the facilitators] gave us this welcome last year and it was to mothers, and daughters, and sisters, and people with disabilities. It was about a fifteen-minute welcome. That's what brought our group together. It just felt like you could say and be anything in that room with no fears at all that we were all equal regardless of white, black, brown, red, sick, healthy.

Other Possible Impacts

We didn't collect data on other possible impacts of the focus on facilitation, but we are learning what to look for. If we were to do it over again, we might look for evidence of better meetings and of increased use of co-facilitation within participating unions, of more participatory SFL courses at other education events, and of more effective design of SFL courses and events overall.

NOW WHAT? LESSONS LEARNED

Leadership Development a Long-Term Commitment

We learned that developing comfort and confidence as a facilitator requires more than giving someone four days of training. We need to offer regular support over a longer period of time, including mentoring, apprenticeships and opportunities to facilitate in low risk situations. We thought that offering facilitation courses to more women would create more women facilitators. But we have learned that other active interventions are needed, post-training, to support the continuing development of as many facilitators as possible. We could have held follow-up conference calls with graduates of the facilitator courses to hear what they were experiencing and to share ideas. We could have, from the beginning, recruited graduates to co-facilitate with more experienced facilitators at other federation of labour events. We could have created an email group of graduates to help them maintain connection and keep them thinking about popular education. All this was, and still is, within our means.

Recruit Diverse Facilitators

School organizers made a point of ensuring that the course on Indigenous issues was facilitated by Indigenous women, that the course on sexual orientation and homophobia was facilitated by lesbians, and that the course about disability rights had at least one facilitator with a disability. Other courses, however, were taught mainly by straight white women. What was needed, but did not take place, was the active recruitment of participants from diverse groups to attend the school in general and the facilitation courses in particular. School organizers could, in the future, set a goal that all courses at each school be co-facilitated by racialized, Indigenous and young women, even if this means inviting women from allied community organizations or other provinces.

Connect Facilitators to the Unions

There was no explicit plan to build bridges between the PSUW's facilitator-development efforts and what was going on for the rest of the year in women's affiliated unions. School organizers left it to individual graduates to go back to their own unions and make a case for involvement in their education programs. That worked for some; but for many, it did not. We wonder now if even a letter to each new facilitator's union, describing what she had accomplished at the school, would have been useful. This is one of the options that could have been explored in explicit conversations with affiliates but was not.

The PSUW also bumped against a union culture of discrete educational events, limited if any follow-up and a narrow notion of the "real business" of the union. Bargaining, arbitration, campaigns and organizing are the priorities of unions; education is seen as nice but not essential. And education is not necessarily understood as part of what actually happens in bargaining, arbitration, campaigns and organizing. Therefore, educators and facilitators are not taken as seriously as grievance officers or health and safety reps. In addition, the practice of discrete educational events, unconnected to the "real business" of the union, has a disproportionate effect on women, racialized and other workers, whose hopes get raised by an event like the PSUW and dashed with the lack of follow-up.

Incorporate Follow-Up Actions

Any or all of the following actions could significantly increase the impact of the PSUW:

- Reframe the school as an ongoing program rather than a one-off annual event.
- Assign someone in the Federation of Labour, at the completion of each annual school, to report to affiliate unions about which of their members

took facilitator training. This might encourage the affiliates to use these new facilitators in their own education programs.

- Make education serve what is seen as the "real business" of the union, and by so doing, bring different perspectives to that business. For example, if a union is running a major health and safety campaign, perhaps its PSUW-trained facilitators could design and facilitate lunch-and-learns or other events to engage members.
- Offer follow-up meetings or calls with graduates to find out what is going on in their unions, how/if they are able to apply their learning in their unions and what supports would be helpful.
- Systematically promote the accomplishments of facilitation-course graduates, especially those who are racialized, Indigenous or young, to their own unions. Talk about them with education staff, staff representatives or elected officers. In some unions, staff are already asked to keep their eye out for emerging stars. This is an existing, informal talent-spotting system that, increasingly, uses an equity lens.
- Hold regular conversations with education staff of participating unions to find out how to increase the likelihood that a PSUW graduate would be asked to facilitate in her own union.
- Explore with participating unions the different ways that skilled facilitators can be beneficial to their organizations.
- Hold events between schools to bring diverse participants together in order to continue to develop and apply their skills. One of these events might be specifically for racialized and Indigenous women facilitators.
- Pay attention to the events calendars of participating unions. For example, offer to report at meetings of the Saskatchewan Federation of Labour Executive Council and of affiliates' executive bodies.

Encourage Emergence of New Facilitators

The founders of the PSUW created two important practices to continuously develop new facilitators. First, the rule of "three years and rest" prevented a small number of women from facilitating the same courses year after year. It required a constant influx of new facilitators trying out new courses or teaching the old ones in different ways. It encouraged experimentation. It made space. When an organization is trying to ensure that more racialized, Indigenous and younger women emerge as leaders, such procedures are crucial.

Second, the facilitator preparation weekend brought people together as a community of educators. Every year it focused on a new theme, and new facilitators attended because of the three-year rule. The facilitator preparation weekend often incubated new ideas for the whole school, not just for individual courses.

At the time of writing, neither of these practices are being followed. The "three years and rest" rule demands more time and effort because school organizers have to monitor who needs to rest each year, imagine a list of possible new candidates and then do the leg work to confirm their availability and orient them to the school. Without a constantly changing cadre of facilitators, the facilitator preparation weekend seems less necessary, because many of the same women, most of them white, are still teaching the same courses. The good news is that it is never too late to resume effective practices.

The Prairie School for Union Women has been, and continues to be, a significant incubator for emerging women educational leaders and for new ideas about union education. We are grateful for the opportunity to have been profoundly influenced by it over the years. And it has been a source of our hope for a movement that can learn from the limits of its trade-offs, the boundaries of its imagination and its enormous successes.

Notes

1. "Popular education," from the Spanish *educación popular*, refers to a form of education developed in the global South which helps groups of people to analyze power relations in their situation in order to act on them collectively as well as individually (Burke et al. 2002: 8, 46).

CHAPTER TWO

FEMINISM AND TRANSFORMATION
The Prairie School for Union Women

Cindy Hanson and Adriane Paavo

One of Saskatchewan's best kept secrets is its feminist, annual labour school for women, the Prairie School for Union Women. For almost three decades, it has been changing lives. The Prairie School for Union Women (PSUW) was organized in the mid-1990s by women activists and staff from Saskatchewan's labour movement. They wanted to promote women's involvement in the labour movement and saw a women-only learning space as an important way to achieve the goal. The PSUW was inspired by women-only schools organized by the British Columbia Federation of Labour together with a regional labour body in the north-western United States.

The first PSUW was held in 1997 and then each year since, with one exception. A typical school brings together about 150 women (participants, facilitators, recreation and wellness staff, on-site coordinators and childcare workers) and ten to fifteen of their children for four days of classes and plenaries. From the beginning, the women who participated — as learners, facilitators and support workers — loved the school. Anecdotal reports abounded of the ways the school energized women and made a difference in their activist lives. Applications always exceeded capacity, a sure sign of success. Until 2009.

In 2009, the school had to be cancelled due to low enrolment. Organizers were very concerned — what had happened? Were "the boys" finally pushing back after twelve years? The answer was no, as it turned out. The low registration numbers were due to a perfect storm of other issues, and the organizers responded by taking steps to get the school back on track. But they realized they needed to do a better job of documenting the work and impact of the school. They had anecdotal evidence of success but wanted something more solid in case they ever needed to defend the school's existence.

As an activist and adult educator, Cindy had a long-standing interest in the school. Adriane, one of the school's founders and organizers, invited her to meet with the school's Steering Committee. That discussion led to two community-university research projects exploring whether the school was increasing women's union activism, solidarity and leadership (Hanson 2012b, 2015) and what practices and structures were triggering that transformation.

Labour education is a form of adult learning that encourages workers to critically analyze their roles in the world, union and workplace "so that lives, workplaces and communities can be transformed" (Carter and Martin 2013: 270). Labour education is increasingly seen as a way to provide tools and spaces so that equity-seeking groups can learn, mobilize and prioritize issues of relevance to their lived conditions as workers and union activists (Ross, Savage, Black and Silver 2015). Women who participated in the research projects clearly described the labour education they experienced at the school as life-altering, often extending beyond personal transformation and into their workplaces and communities.

Laurie (not her real name) is a middle-aged Indigenous woman who attended the school once, taking a course called Everyday Activism. Laurie repeatedly described how the school broadened her view of issues from a purely individual effect to a collective impact:

> I'm a lot more accepting that I was before … I went to the Prairie School for Women and I walked away from there realizing that there's a lot more that affects me, but I just don't see it, 'cause I'm not seeing it. I'm walking around with blinders…. 'Cause when you walk out of the school you start seeing things as a bigger picture about how all these issues affect everybody and even though it affects them differently, it really affects everybody in the same way…. you realize you're fighting for all your sisters. You know, it's not about you; it's about everybody.

The participants recognized that the school's education methodology was central to the impact.

FEMINIST POPULAR EDUCATION

To understand how the school tries to achieve its goals, it is useful to pause and look at approaches to emancipatory, critical adult learning, which are the stated cornerstones of the PSUW's methodology. Transformative education was significantly shaped by the work of Brazilian educator Paulo Freire (1970) and his concept of *educaçao popular* (popular education). Popular education principles and techniques are used in labour education, for example, to deepen consciousness building and increase workers' awareness of oppression and their rights (Carter and Martin 2013).

Feminists extended popular education's power analysis from social class alone to other forms of oppression, such as gender, race and ability (Manicom and Walters 2012). The courses taught at the school are designed and instructed using the theory and practice or praxis models that emerge from Freirian goals of educating for social change. The PSUW places diverse women's experiences at the heart of all of its courses, a feminist approach that some argue is missing from labour education and union renewal (Briskin 2006; Kainer 2006). For example, women's work roles are recognized as central to how the school structures programs — it prioritizes not only course time, but recreation and wellness. As well, the school's practices of offering mentorship, free on-site childcare and scholarships for women from equity-seeking groups are some of the other ways it applies a feminist approach outside the classroom.

The PSUW overturned gendered access to labour education in Saskatchewan. During the annual school, courses provide over twenty hours of instruction in various union- and social-justice-related topics, including feminism and trade unionism, Indigenous issues, collective bargaining, homophobia, dis/abilities, popular education skills, advocacy and protest, and gender dimensions of the workplace. Course names such as Well-Behaved Women Seldom Make History, Women Speaking Out, and What Colour Is a Union? illustrate both breadth in social-justice programming as well as the women- or equality-centred content. All courses are designed using popular-education methods and principles. And courses are also expected to have a feminist analysis and investigate intersecting issues of identity and inequality. By doing so, school organizers state, courses can look at different forms of discrimination and privilege based on gender, race, class, age, ability and other identity characteristics so that women are not treated as one homogeneous group (Paavo 2001).

The school's Steering Committee, a partner in the research discussed in this chapter, included staff from the Saskatchewan Federation of Labour and a volunteer group of past participants and facilitators. They met to plan the annual school and tried to ensure that the courses and approaches to learning and operations remained feminist-centred (although feminist is not explicitly defined).

RESEARCHING COLLABORATIVELY, *FOR* AND *WITH* THE WOMEN

Because the PSUW is dedicated to amplifying the voices of women workers, we used feminist participatory action research methods to ensure the results were developed with the PSUW community and that attention was paid to the agency and voices of the women who participated. Women union members shaped the research projects, and their opinions determined the outcomes.

First of all, the PSUW Steering Committee and researchers met to determine what key questions the committee wanted to answer. And the committee defined the target group for research participants, spread the word about the research and encouraged school learners to volunteer to take part, including by allowing the researchers to hold focus group sessions at the school itself. During the course of the research, the Steering Committee and the researchers met and communicated regularly to ensure ongoing feedback into the research process. Eventually, a facilitated workshop was used to share the findings with the Steering Committee. They ranked the recommendations to reach consensus on priorities for action and implementation.

The research methods included an analysis of past program brochures and participant evaluations, particularly from the previous five years. And we held individual interviews and focus groups with thirty-seven women who had participated at the school as learners or, in a few cases, as facilitators. (One participant chose to be interviewed by telephone; another responded to our interview questions in writing.)

The research participants were a diverse group and generally representative of the range of women union members who attend the school. They were women aged twenty-four to sixty-five, from a range of unions, class backgrounds, sexual orientations, geographies and races. Several self-identified as belonging to an equity-seeking group, specifically Indigenous, differently abled, lesbian and youth. Most were rank-and-file union members, while a few were staff of unions. At least one study participant mentioned attending the school through its scholarship program. Some research participants had attended the school for the first time, while others were returning participants (from as far back as the first school in 1997). All research participants chose or were given pseudonyms, to provide as much confidentiality as possible.

WHAT TRIGGERS TRANSFORMATION?

Women told us that the school is meeting its goals of building solidarity and increasing women's involvement in union activism and union leadership. They spoke about feeling hopeful, inspired and rejuvenated as a result of their participation in the school. Mani said in a focus group: "It really opened up an inner part of me that I didn't realize was locked up." Another participant wrote on her evaluation form: "I discovered I am a feminist and gained the confidence to become involved and no longer be just one of the boys." The women in our research projects were describing personal and political changes brought about by learning environments that build confidence and promote sharing and solidarity among learners, an experience noted by other researchers (Kirton and Healy 2004). The women also described the school as a place where they could explore subjects they had not considered previously. Janet stated:

I've never been to anything like this in my life and it's just opened my eyes hugely to not only women's issues, but the history of the union. I'm embarrassed to say I've been a union member for thirty years, but taking night school, got married, had two babies all the while working full time.... Just the environment has been, [sighs] I just feel so safe and loved and validated, and what I'm learning is transforming conflict, is just something I can use in my whole life.

Of course it is not enough to know that learners found a learning event or methodology to be transformative. We wanted to explore how, concretely, does the PSUW (and women-only schools or union learning in general) encourage women's leadership and bring about the transformation of a woman worker into someone who takes action for social justice? The PSUW participants who took part in the research were insightful about what triggered their transformation. We grouped their responses into four categories: 1) design and facilitation choices; 2) environment outside of the classroom; 3) the women-only nature of the school; and 4) logistical arrangements and organizational choices.

Design and Facilitation Choices

There was an obvious but encouraging conclusion from this research: Course content can play a significant role in creating the conditions for transformation. This includes the design choices made before a learning event as well as the deliberate or spontaneous choices facilitators make on their feet once an event is underway, for example in how they engage with and respond to learners. Research participants talked about the positive impact of course content that is relevant to their lives and that is presented through practical, hands-on activities. Julia observed that taking part in activities which drew on participants' actual work lives helped her feel more courageous: "It's because when we start doing some of the exercises it looks like what I would hear when I was working and I [previously] didn't know how to deal with that."

Building opportunities for self-reflection into course content was important for Esther, as she compared her PSUW experience to another labour school: "That's another big difference between [the other school] and Prairie School ... there isn't a lot of that kind of time for self-reflection and remembering to give yourself a pat on the back, not just other people."

When facilitators take the time to fully welcome participants at the beginning of a course, they create the trust, comfort and openness necessary for transformation to take place. Celia said:

I think that's what brought our group together. By the end of that welcome it just felt like you could say and be anything in that room with no fears at all, that we were all equal regardless of white, black, brown, red, sick, healthy. I really can't say I've experienced it any-

21

where else like that. Like I've been judged quite a bit 'cause I'm a very passionate speaker.

Lucy noted that the safe, welcoming environment allowed for relationship-building:

> Being a First Nations woman, you're very careful about what you tell people or how open you are to somebody. I mean you only give people surface stuff and that's it. By the second day I was discussing things with people that I wouldn't in a million years have even dreamed of discussing with a person I'd never even met before ... we spent half the day just getting to know each other and who was in the room and what we did and what made us who we are and like I can't remember exactly all the steps that they went through but by the end of the day, like I said, we all felt like we were almost family ... you know, the trust thing.

Something as simple as setting ground rules for respectful participation can be a significant signal for some learners, as Tina described:

> Knowing that it matters what I say and what I feel and if, you know, a whole twenty other women can accept what I say and don't cut me down, darn it all, you who belong in the same local as me can listen to me. So, it's powerful. I mean if they had cut me down the way I was used to being cut down it would have been a total negative experience and I wouldn't want to go back.

According to research participants, the most significant curricular choice made by course designers and facilitators was incorporating personal storytelling activities. As Tina noted, having others listen to one's story is an empowering experience. Many other research participants linked their transformation to storytelling which engaged their emotions or built connections and community among participants:

> One person would tell the story and you actually could relate to that person and what they're saying. Then everybody starts relating in their own little way and then everybody starts sharing how they relate to that and how it affects their life and how they relate to that. It becomes like a whole big picture story, you know like about how you start seeing the whole picture, but how it affects everybody. You actually become a community and a family rather than just an individual person that's trying to sit there and take a pen and paper and learn something. (Laurie)

Powerful storytelling inspired other listeners to take action, as Esther explains:

> So, you can't be in a class like that and not be impacted. Those stories will always stick in my mind. "If they can do that, what can I do?" ... I just found as things presented itself over the next few years where possibly I would have shied away from it, I didn't. So, it [the PSUW course] had immediate effects and then long term.

Esther attended the PSUW several times and had a deeper analysis about the use of storytelling. She noted that not all course topics lent themselves to deeper, emotional discussions, and sometimes those that do present other challenges:

> I was just emotionally drained actually, and not dreading going to the class at all, but just feeling the heaviness of the memories. When you hear stories like that, you're never going to get rid of them. You're lucky if you don't dream about them.

Clearly, storytelling can be a powerful tool when used skillfully and compassionately by facilitators.

Environment Outside of the Classroom

While course designers and facilitators played a key role in creating conditions for transformative learning inside the classroom, research participants identified another category of conditions that lead to transformation: the school's environment outside the classroom.

Messages of inclusion and welcome are ubiquitous at the school, from the moment participants arrive on-site: "When you're at the school it's pretty much mentioned almost every day, so it just stays in your forefront" (Esther). Organizers deliberately design opening-day activities and recreational events to make sure no one feels left out or at loose ends.

Perhaps influenced by these activities and messages, other participants also contributed to this feeling of belonging with their supportive behaviours, as Laurie described:

> The girls that had been there a couple of times, they make sure, if you're sitting like a wallflower other there, that ain't happening. "You're coming sitting over here!" and they're introducing you to everybody and they're "Oh, you gotta try this" or, "We've going to go over to the taco place."

Camille identified something similar:

It's truly a feeling of not just being supported, whether it's at the supper table or in the classroom, but [also the] knowledge in the classroom just learning from women…. So much sharing and so much learning and that can be right down to talking about your children and parenting them, or your relationship issues or whatever conversations that you get into. You get sort of close with those women that it feels safe. [Another participant interjects: It's like acceptance.] Yeah it is, it is.

Besides overcoming barriers between strangers — such as those arising from race and age — the welcoming nature of the school helped overcome stereotypes unique to the labour movement: those based on which union one belongs to. Iris observed that the school helped participants see one another as people first:

And then you find out behind the stigma of being a [worker in a specific industry] is what a great person she is and how easy she was to talk to. You leave all the rest of that stuff behind. Prejudice and bias because of some controversial issue or anything like that…. It's sort of like when you pay for your gate pass [at the entrance of the national park where the Prairie School for Union Women has been held since 2005], you're leaving it there. Pick it up on the way out 'cause you still have to deal with it, but you leave it there, right?

Marianne saw a clear link between this inclusive environment and learning:

The class actually didn't stop at 4:30. The class moved itself out of the building at 4:30 and it very much carried on into every activity. For myself, when I thought I couldn't do something, it's like, "Wait a minute … someone will pick me up if I fall," and I felt safe enough to try different things.

Larning in a safe place helped participants believe they could take action and then follow through:

You're speaking and doing speeches in front of the women every time that it actually makes you feel like, "Oh wow, I can do it in front of strangers." (Cassandra)

[Unions were] like a foreign language. And so were politics, to be perfectly honest…. [The PSUW] was a safe place for me to learn about politics, understand even the parties and their platforms, and I didn't feel stupid or foolish. So, I got involved this time around, talking about the election and phoned my local NDP representative ... and said, "Absolutely you can put a sign in my yard." Yup, became very much more involved in what was going on and trying to explain to other people that [politics] as well as the union. (Camille)

Women-Only Nature of the School

Anne-Marie Greene and Gill Kirton (2002) describe women-only labour education as a lifeline for sustaining and expanding women's union activism. Such schools help women develop confidence to pursue activism beyond the workplace. Women at the PSUW described having the same experience.

Research participants were quick to point out that the school was unlike other labour education that privileged an "old boys' club." In particular, women said that the school felt like a safe space where they could speak up and not be judged. For Dora, the school helped keep her active in the union movement when she might have stopped, because of her triple workload:

> The timing of [the school] was really good... To be dealing with stuff at home, at work, union, you know, you'd just be facing issue after issue after issue, so kind of on the flip side of it I think that the school can motivate and encourage me to keep going and fighting [laughs] you know, patriarchy and the whole bit.

One participant who took the course Transforming Conflict repeatedly spoke about how it gave her confidence to make demands of her union:

> After the course I got, I was feeling pretty strong about what I could do for my co-workers as a steward ... and this is why I went to my union and I said, "Please, I need another course" ... But this time I feel very, very confident. (Julia)

Women within the union movement emphasize the importance of women-only schools as one key to union renewal (Briskin, Genge, McPhail and Pollack 2013), and most of our research participants shared that sentiment.

Logistical Arrangements and Organizational Choices

Research participants said the way the school was structured helped them connect with other women, hold relevant conversations and learn. Holding the school at Waskesiu, a resort town in a national park some distance from any major centre, prevented other work and family demands from interfering. Offering on-site childcare as part of the school set-up was mentioned as important on many occasions. Esther noted its significance:

> I'm hoping it will continue to be just extremely impactful for myself and my kids. Because there's no dad to help out with anything or

interfere or [laughing] whatever there is that day.... In addition, it's a great opportunity for me to take my kids to something union-based and for them to grow up with that language and those outlooks and that experience and they talk about it all year long. All year long.... You know they love being with the kids there. They love the safe, free, accepting environment.... I think it will show my son and my daughter that you know, unions are important and they're great places to be and we have lifelong memories about it too.

Research participants also mentioned that the daily morning plenaries, which bring all participants together, and the presence of women from many different unions made them feel open to new learning and to personal change.

RECOMMENDATIONS FROM THE RESEARCH

We presented the results of the research to the PSUW's Steering Committee in 2014, along with a series of "Recommendations for Building and Sustaining Transformation." We drew some of the recommendations from research participants' descriptions of their transformation and from their opinions of what caused it. And some recommendations came from the research participants themselves. The women we interviewed provided suggestions about how the school could keep alive their feelings of empowerment and their resolutions to behave in new ways back in "the real world." Recommendations fell into three main areas: supporting and guiding course designers and facilitators; creating programs to deliberately maintain new behaviours and attitudes; and using communications tools to deliberately maintain new behaviours and attitudes.

The school's Steering Committee is its governing body, making key decisions about its structure and program. Any prairie-based union woman who is interested can serve on this committee. And as a powerful partner in the participatory research process, the committee could decide to accept and implement, re-interpret or reject any of the recommendations presented. The committee did accept most recommendations related to communications and support for course designers and facilitators. It accepted some recommendations about creating programs to deliberately maintain transformed behaviours and attitudes. It would be fair to say the committee's decisions were sometimes affected by the potential cost and difficulty of implementation — particularly implementation outside the annual four-day time and space of the school. Some of the recommendations accepted by the Steering Committee included:

- equip course designers and facilitators with tools to build storytelling activities into courses;

- inoculate women for re-entering the reality of the outside world, such as providing them with tips for dealing with disillusionment, push-back from others and loss of self-confidence;
- create "learning buddies" or "learning triads": other learners with whom women will stay in touch post-school;
- establish a mentoring system between former and new school attendees; and
- create a (voluntary) directory at each school of participants' names, contact information and areas of specialization/expertise.

The Steering Committee determined that some recommendations were not a priority for action, including: 1) holding a shorter educational event each year midway between schools where past participants can reconnect and take stock of personal and collective progress; 2) encouraging unions to send at least two participants from any union local (since creating "learning buddies" is one way to increase the chances that transformation will be sustained); and 3) building in meeting time (face-to-face or online) for facilitators to debrief after the school and build upon lessons learned.

CONCLUSION

The PSUW research filled gaps in the understanding of how women-only labour schools trigger and sustain transformation. The women we talked to believed that attending the school had changed them for the better. They developed confidence and were personally transformed. That transformation was triggered by the methods used to design and facilitate school courses, by the school's environment inside and outside the classroom, and by logistical choices, including the creation of spaces for women learners only. The PSUW has employed these practices to good effect, particularly during the week that the school is in session.

However, the women who took part in the research pointed out how challenges arose when they left the school and had to maintain their new self-image or resolutions for action, often without much support. Our research provided many recommendations for changing practices in order to sustain transformation. Time will show if and how they can be put into action, and if and how they achieve results. It is clear that efforts beyond the school alone are required before union women can transform union culture and achieve equality. The PSUW brings a critical mass of union women one step closer to those goals. Further progress will depend on how well the PSUW is able to reconstruct itself as the start, not the end, of a process of transformation.

CHAPTER THREE

UNION WOMEN ON TURTLE ISLAND
A Conversation

Sandra Ahenekew and Yvonne Hotzak, interviewed by Cindy Hanson

Even today, few unions or labour schools teach courses about Indigenous views and history. When the Saskatchewan Federation of Labour's Aboriginal Committee commissioned the creation of the course Unionism on Turtle Island, it was breaking important new ground. Designed by D'Arcy Martin and Barb Thomas, with active participation by committee members and other Indigenous trade unionists, the course was piloted it in 2001. A few years later, organizers of the Prairie School for Union Women asked two of the Indigenous women facilitators to offer the course, with an increased focus on gender. Union Women on Turtle Island has been taught at the school each year since.

Both the original course and the women's course aim to deepen workers' understanding of the impact of Canada's colonial history on Indigenous Peoples, to look at Indigenous Peoples' ongoing efforts to resist and thrive, and to build greater capacity for solidarity (and allies) by workers and unions with these struggles.

Yvonne and Sandra are two women who recently facilitated the women's course. This chapter contains their voices (transcribed from an interview conducted by Cindy Hanson), as they reflect on why the course is successful; how it integrates Indigenous knowledge, history, storytelling and even humour; and what some of the challenges are. The discussion provides lessons for labour educators, popular educators, and others who are trying to grasp how Canada's colonial history affects Indigenous women and how to put reconciliation into action.

***

Yvonne: I am a registered nurse. I'm with the Saskatchewan Union of Nurses. I've been with the Prairie School for probably for about ten years. I missed one year in there, I don't know which year it was, but I've been teaching [Union Women on] Turtle Island for four years with Sandra. I think the first course I ever took was that one, and it was so impressive that I just kept coming back.

Sandra: I'm Sandra Ahenakew and I work for Indigenous and Northern Affairs Canada [Indigenous Services Canada]. I've been with this department for about seventeen years now. I've been involved with a union about that long. Fifteen years ago I took a [Public Service] Alliance [of Canada (PSAC)] facilitator training course with Judy Shannon, who sparked something in me, and I took the Turtle Island course shortly after that. I've been facilitating at Prairie School, it feels like a very long time, but maybe eight years. I've also facilitated and co-facilitated with PSAC staff.

I have never attended Prairie School for Union Women as a participant. So, I've only ever gone as a facilitator and I've only been about eight years. It's just been in the last four years that they have invited Yvonne and I. I think it's because we work well together, and we get some really awesome feedback from participants. They love us, but it's not really us, I believe. I believe what they love is the learning experience and the journey that we assist them with. And I think that that's what they love. They love our storytelling style.

Yvonne: I'd like to add a little something: that we are very flexible in what happens in our course. Each year it's done, is not identical. We are flexible with whatever is happening with our class.... I think it depends on who's attending. I think when we first started together, there were more Caucasian ladies, and then it was more Aboriginal girls, and now it's more of a half-half thing.... The Aboriginal girls do not know their own history, and I think that's part of why there are so many suicides and they need to learn their own history. We don't have enough education in the schools.

Sandra: We hear from the participants all the time that they've been trying to get into the course for years.... I think you know we have twelve to fifteen at the most, at Prairie School [courses], so it's a fairly small group. And as you know, it's popular education and people sharing their experiences and their knowledge, and that allows us as facilitators to kind of see at what level are they. Where do we need to take them? The biggest thing I think is the [historical] time-line exercise and the opportunity for storytelling within there. I think that we get the best feedback on that particular exercise and some of the videos that we use as well.

I think [popular education is] recognizing that every individual comes with their knowledge and their experiences, their life experience. So they're not just starting at scratch and not everybody is starting at the same level. Through discussion and sharing and using a variety of tools, we can target different people's learning needs. Whether it's small group exercises, activities that get them up and moving or watching videos, listening to music. But finding a way to tap into the needs of the learners, and that changes with every person that is in the room. You want to make sure that every single individual that is part of the course has an opportunity to learn in a way that they can accept this knowledge that we're trying to share with them. Some people like to touch and read things. Some people like to hear things. Some people like to stand up and do things. It's recognizing the different needs of the learners. Popular education is really sharing and making sure that everybody is included and that we're not separating people.

Yvonne: We also take them on that journey. We take them to a zone where they're uncomfortable because that's where a lot of learning happens. [For example] it might be the Kanesatake[1] story or the story for many of the Indian residential school survivors.

Sandra: Yeah. So, the [Indian] residential schools are huge, right, with the Truth and Reconciliation hearings. We take them on an emotional journey. I know this sounds sad, but we want them to feel, and to feel it in their hearts, because that's what moves you to action, when you are touched by something. When they're hearing those stories and the Kanesatake is, although it's almost a thirty-year-old story of resistance from the Mohawk people and Canada's reaction to that. So they get to experience it.

Yvonne was saying we take them out of their comfort zone. The comfort zone is at the core where everything's all good. But learning happens in the discomfort zone. So that's where we want them to be. We need them to be uncomfortable. We need them to feel their emotions: to feel angry, to feel sad, to feel hurt. At the end, what we do is: "Now what can we do?" And we show them ways that they can go back to their workplaces. I think we have to make them stronger as unionists and also as allies.

Sandra: I agree. We give them our contact information so they're able to contact us and to ask us questions. For example, one of the participants from this past year, she was very touched and moved by what she learned. And she wanted to bring it to her [union] local and was looking for us to share with her the myths and misconceptions exercise. She wanted something she could do for a lunch-and-learn. Then she was going to bring it to her regional women's committee. She was motivated. I mean, that's kind of what we want to do, right? We want to spark some interest in them. And she's a non-Indigenous woman who was very happy to have learned about the history.

The time-line exercise — we start from prior to contact and we explain to them that this is how the Indigenous peoples were living at that time. We show them a short video from PSAC, called *Justice for Aboriginal People*. It's a five-minute video that goes quickly over a large part of history. They get a little brief history of prior to contact — this is how it was — and then we start introducing contact. Through storytelling about different events in history, different studies that were done, when the Indian Act was introduced, when treaties were introduced. And this seems to be an exercise that has consistently given us really good feedback from the participants.

Yvonne: I feel like we don't just stand up and talk, talk, talk. We want as much participation as possible from our audience. And also, to teach the courses, we are both Aboriginal, and I think it's difficult for someone else to try and teach our people. You know what I mean? We also use an opening circle and a closing circle, the talking stick. We bring a lot of cultural values into what we do, and prayer.

Sandra: Smudging.

Yvonne: Yeah, smudging. Lots of things like that. If they have bad feelings from the day before, we can talk about it. We can get them cleared up. There's a lot of healing that happens within our circles and within our course as well.

Some of the girls are really hurt about something. We get them to talk about it and we try and make them feel better about everything. About what's happening. Like even the Kanesatake thing — that is Canadian, but that also affects many things in our world like Standing Rock in the States. It's just a different decade that it happened in.

The healing ... we've even had participants who have expressed feelings of suicide before coming to the school. The course helped her understand her history and who she was, and she felt better after taking the course. I think that we did help her.

Sandra: It was very hard to hear stories like this one. But we talk about the protocol with the circle and understanding that when a person is holding the talking stick we're all engaged in listening and there's no interrupting. So, I mean it was hard to hear but very uplifting at the same time too, to know that the information that we had presented to her was helping her and giving her some of the answers she needed. And she no longer felt like she had no purpose. It is a very tough course.

This last year was very hard for both Yvonne and me. We didn't get to really complete a lot of things because one of our — we call them *little turtles*, right, that's just what I've been calling the participants for years — one of the women lost her daughter tragically. We had just finished the [KAIROS] blanket exercise. So we didn't get to de-brief our group.... When we heard that this woman had lost her daughter, everything just kind of stopped. We had to re-evaluate. How do you get back on track when this has happened to your group?

Yvonne: They didn't want to do their presentations, so we did a different one. We were just flexible about everything. And that's where the flexibility comes in. We just go with the flow and try and make things work.

Sandra: It's important for people to get up and move around and stuff, and some people are very visual. So the blanket exercise really touches them on another level. Particularly those participants that get the envelopes. "You're a child that has been taken from your home to go to a residential school. Step off the blanket and you are no longer on Turtle Island." "You have been infected with smallpox. Step off the blanket because you've died." It's the physical movement.[2] And you see how much the land has shrunk from being the whole country to a very small portion of it, that that's all we really have now. We try to do our recap within our closing circle as well.

Yvonne: The KAIROS blanket exercise reinforces the time-line that we did. So we do the time-line before we get to the blanket exercise. That's a good one.

Sandra: We talk about our personal experiences as Indigenous Peoples. Speaking from a place of knowing. For example, what it's like for myself to grow up on reserve. Like when we talk about Indian control of Indian education, we're dealing with the issue of the 1969 White Paper, and the [Indigenous] reaction to that was the Red Paper. I tell them about the day when we were all bussed from the reserves into the small towns to go to school. And one day the buses came, and they pulled all of us Indian kids off, out of the schools. And that's when schools started being built on reserves. We started teaching our children ourselves, you know? So I'm able to tell them from a place of knowing.

A big part of Indigenous history and culture is our oral stories and storytelling. They're not fables that we're sharing. We're sharing experiences and other people's stories that we've heard. Yvonne has personal knowledge of traumatic things that happened to her family that she shares as well. So, although people might think that these events we're talking about are things that happened in the past, what we're showing them is that it is still happening. It happened to me. It's happening to my grandchildren. The storytelling is a huge part of the Turtle Island course.

We're really just trying to give them tools and show them how Canadian society, journalism, the government, how they continue to perpetuate these ideas, and to get the participants to start asking "Why?" Who benefits from not having this in the curriculum, or from not presenting true stories within the media? Then they can start looking at the stories and asking questions.

We talk about treaties and we look at it in the context of negotiating a collective agreement.... Within the time-line we try to show them that the union has struggled for their rights and the things that we have within the collective agreement. We try to show them how the Indigenous Peoples have continued to resist. They've been attacked throughout history, and they've continued to resist throughout history and to this day. It's like Yvonne said: sometimes it takes a while for the light bulb to come on with some of them [participants]. Or to break down what their truths are, like things that their grandparents have said, that their husband or their in-laws or their family, or you know, their community made them believe. Their long-held beliefs that are based on untruth. Trying to peel that back in a safe way so that we're not hurting them. We don't want to damage people. But we want them to come to their own understanding and learning.

Cindy: I love the analogy that you just brought up — the analogy of collective bargaining and treaty-making. Looking at treatymaking like collective bargaining — where you have to struggle, and you have to get through these differences in ideas and come to a place of reconciliation.

Yvonne: [We talk about the similarities between collective bargaining and treaty-making], except with the treaties we had, our people had a different understanding of what they actually meant, and they agreed to it not knowing what they were agreeing to. You know what I'm saying there.

Sandra: I do, Yvonne. It is a really good exercise for people. I mean the whole point, I think, is that we're trying to build union activists, so we do our best to try and incorporate and show them the similarities. You know, as unionists we struggled to have our rights recognized, occupational health and safety in a workplace, whatever those were. But to understand that the Indigenous Peoples used ceremonies and the ceremonies went on prior to treaty-signing. That this was an agreement that was between three parties, the understanding of the Indigenous Peoples was that it was between the Creator, the Queen's representative, and the Indigenous Peoples. It wasn't just about the words. It was about spirit and intent. You know, it wasn't being locked down into the words, but once you sign, it's [sacred]. And once you sign a contract, it's signed. We signed away our severance; it's gone; it's not coming back. So, trying to let them see that we struggle together.

But what we're trying [to do] at the end of the day is to build allies, and people that will go out there and, you know, talk to their MPs and MLAs. Talk about the missing and murdered Indigenous women. Talk about truth and reconciliation and the calls to action. "Let's do this." And I think that's what we've done. For every time that we facilitate that course, we are putting ripples throughout Turtle Island. There are people leaving the course with a small little shell of knowledge, but they go forth and they start looking and asking. And they start questioning, and that's what we want them to do.

Yvonne: We get the participants to help facilitate the course also. Those who know something also give that to us in the course. Well, everyone gives the information that they have. We had one particular girl this last time who took a lot of training with the women elders where she's from. And she brought us some information that I didn't know before.

Sandra: Like a lot of the cultural teaching. It actually happens quite a lot when we're fortunate enough to have those people that practise oral traditions or their traditions and culture. When we're fortunate enough to have one of them in the group, they can explain things like why we smudge, what does smudging mean.

And I think it's important, as part of reconciliation, for us to recognize that we are on the traditional territory of Indigenous Peoples of Turtle Island. So, wherever we happen to be, the first thing that we do is recognize the traditional territory of, like, right now I'm sitting in Treaty Four territory in Regina. We let them know that that's a simple thing that you can do.... We have so many materials and so many exercises but not enough time to do them all.

A lot of the women are mothers, so in talking about residential schools we tell them imagine somebody is coming, like the police are coming, and they're going to take your four- or five-year-old child away from you and there's nothing that you can do about it. It's tough, it's very tough. Because sometimes they cry, and we can't let them leave or the circle is broken. So we try to bring them back and to promise them that it's important and what they're feeling is exactly what they need to be feeling, but that we're not going to let you leave this place feeling hopeless and broken because at the end of the day, we want you to be motivated. You felt it. You're ready to put your boots to the ground. [Union Women on] Turtle Island does that for everybody that's ever taken it. There are also people that have strong beliefs in God and the church. I've had Indigenous People who have left because they can't handle listening to what the church did, and they refuse to accept it. So they've left the room and left the training because they don't want to listen to that. So, I mean, we have to respect people's beliefs. It's pretty hard to tiptoe around the Indian residential school portion of the course.

Yvonne: And we have had people say, "I wasn't going to take this, I wasn't

ready for it. And now here I am because my name got drawn for the class."
We had a girl whose aunt was one of the nuns in residential school, and she
was so happy at the end. She was crying in the beginning and she told us
right away about that. She wasn't ready to talk about the residential schools,
but she was glad she did in the end.

Sandra: I think for Yvonne and me, agreeing to facilitate is always a gift.
When they invite us, I always feel so thankful because this is our small part
in reconciliation. The calls to action, they're near and dear to me. And I
think having Yvonne as a partner to facilitate this and to see reconciliation
in action happening right in front of you, it's so powerful.

Yvonne: I agree. And Sandra is very good at bringing the girls back with her
humour also. Sandra is a bit of a comedian. She tells a lot of personal stories
to most of them. Bringing them back [from hard parts] with that humour.
Just to put a little bit of a laugh in every once in a while, because we can't
have everyone all upset all the time.

Sandra: [Union Women on Turtle Island] is very political and I think we have
to recognize too that, although Canada has thrown all of us Indigenous
Peoples into one pile, that we are very distinct people. The languages. The
cultures.... So it's pretty hard to throw us all in one and then to give us three
and a half days to facilitate the history of Indigenous People and incorporate
all of that. There's much more that needs to be done, but who is it that said,
"The journey starts with the first step." That's what [Union Women on]
Turtle Island is for a lot of people. It's their first step into acknowledging
their ignorance. Now they're no longer ignorant. It's like they have a little
bit of knowledge and sometimes that's dangerous because a movement starts
from a little bit of knowledge.

Yvonne: One of the first questions that we have asked everyone is if they even
know where Turtle Island is, because many people don't know. They think
it's a lake somewhere or an island somewhere. We also discuss who we are. I
am Cree also, but I was an adopted child. My mom was Cree. But I was not
raised that way. I found out later, and once I found out, my family brought
me in as one of their own as I should have been. That's where I did all my
learning, at my mother's feet.

Sandra: My father was a non-Indigenous person. He was Irish. My mother
was Cree. Because I was born before my parents got married, the instant my
mom married my dad she was no longer an Indian. So I was a 6-1, which is
part of the Indian Act. Section 6, subsection 1. I had full status and I'm an

Indian as the Department of Indian Affairs defines it. So my mom was no longer an Indian and my brother, exactly the same parents, who was born after they got married, was a non-Indian. This is part of the storytelling that I'm able to do with people. People are baffled when they find out we're born Indigenous, but the Indian Act and different amendments change that. If you went to university, you were no longer an Indian. If you fought in the wars, you weren't. If you got a university education, you weren't. If you married a non-Indigenous person, you weren't. What's the difference? If my dad had been an Indian and my mom had been the non-Indian, it would have been that my mom would have been an Indian now.

The Sixties Scoop is huge again. But there are people who haven't heard of that. These are the types of things that we're letting them know, and we tell them, here's how you write to your Member of Parliament. We don't want people to feel guilty. That's not it. I mean, we didn't do this. Our ancestors did. But we want to ask: "What are we going to do to make this world a better place?"

Notes

1. Kanesatake is a Mohawk community in southern Quebec where a conflict erupted in 1990 between settlers who wanted to build a golf course and the local Mohawk people, who had a cemetery on the land and considered it sacred.
2. KAIROS blanket exercise — KAIROS: Canadian Ecumenical Justice Initiatives, 1997, revised 2016: "The Blanket Exercise," Toronto, ON.

CHAPTER FOUR

CONFRONTING LIMITS, PUSHING BOUNDARIES
LGBTQ Education and Activism

Donna Smith

Activism is born from the things that we care about and that we believe need to change for our lives and our communities. — Monica Ramirez, co-founder and president of Alianza Nacional de Campesinas

This quote resonates with me. I was not always a social justice activist, but I have spent my whole career working for the labour movement, which is a social movement. My work was always focused on fighting for equality and for the underdog. I am not afraid of challenging injustice and fighting for people who are treated unfairly. I am a feminist through and through, and when I changed job positions and became more knowledgeable about injustices, I could not understand why so much inequality and discrimination existed. In this chapter, I explain the history of lesbian, gay, bisexual, transgender and queer (LGBTQ) activism in the labour movement, how it affected labour education and specifically how one women-only course helped break down stereotypes about the LGBTQ community.

BACKGROUND TO MY STORY

I was raised not really knowing gay or lesbian people. I only heard negative comments and knew nothing about that community. I grew up being a tomboy, knowing I was a bit different and not realizing why. I didn't like feminine things — I liked sports and playing with the boys. I ended up living in a small town, getting married and having three wonderful children. It was what my world expected me to do. Eventually I met people from the LGBTQ community and realized there were people who did not fit gender-stereotyped roles and lived regular lives except they preferred to have relationships with people from their own gender. My marriage lasted ten years before I realized that wasn't the life I was intended to live. In 1989, I packed up my kids and moved to a larger centre. It wasn't easy, but I have few regrets and am a much better person for living my true life.

Besides my lived experience, my focus on LGBTQ activism started in 1997 in Ottawa, when the Canadian Labour Congress hosted a conference specifically for LGBTQ workers. It brought together over three hundred participants from across the country, representing many unions and with varying levels of activism and experience. We discussed issues such as homophobia, legal decisions, negotiating strategies, collective agreement language and creating safe spaces. It was amazing to be both lesbian and working class and able to exchange ideas and experiences. I felt like a sponge — the speakers, the workshops, the environment, the feeling of safety. It was so empowering to hear people's personal stories, talking about their challenges and their struggles, the discrimination they faced and ultimately, some of the wins. I was in awe and knew that coming from a place of privilege — white, employed, member of an organization with a voice — I needed and wanted to bring ideas back to Saskatchewan and fight for equality for the LGBTQ community there.

SFL SOLIDARITY AND PRIDE COMMITTEE

When I returned to Saskatchewan, I approached Barb Byers, then president of the Saskatchewan Federation of Labour (SFL), and asked if I could form a Solidarity and Pride Committee at the SFL. Barb was encouraging and helped me with a presentation to the SFL executive. I was nervous speaking to a predominately male, white, straight, able-bodied executive. I honestly don't remember what I said — something that embodied "I'm here and I'm queer" and our community could use labour's help.

In order to create the committee, we had to ignore traditional practices. Typically, a committee had to be chaired by someone from the executive board, but there was no one on the board who was openly gay. Unless someone was prepared to "come out," I needed approval to chair the committee. Barb realized that sometimes rules need to be ignored. Because she felt this was so important, she convinced the executive that I could chair the committee from outside its ranks, but regularly report back to it and to the SFL annual convention.

The first committee was created from the bottom up. I contacted people I knew who were in a union and presented them with the idea of joining the Solidarity and Pride Committee. This of course meant they needed to talk to their own unions and request permission to join the committee. This was a barrier for some who were not open about their sexual orientation at work or were nervous about being out in their unions. The committee ended up having more women than men, and I believe it was because, in the labour movement and in society in general, it is often safer for women to be out.

The committee grew over the years, with representatives from more unions across the province, and it has had successes including involvement in the fight for spousal benefits and same-sex marriages in Saskatchewan. As well, the committee submitted resolutions for debate at every SFL convention, which meant a commitment to have a speaker in favour of those resolutions at a microphone in front of 600-plus delegates. I became that person, and it was nerve-wracking — sometimes my hand would shake so much I could barely read the speaking notes I was holding.

One occasion I remember clearly is being at a microphone near a group of delegates who were quietly heckling me as I spoke. Supportive people anticipated this reaction and stood beside me in a show of solidarity. Their support made me feel much safer and empowered and showed the convention that our committee had lots of support! It became easier and easier to speak on resolutions, partly because of greater self-confidence but also because it was becoming more politically incorrect to be openly against gay rights. Convention resolutions are an educational tool bringing a broader perspective to the issues themselves by generating discussion.

We also pushed the labour movement to be much more supportive of pride issues in general and to participate in pride parades in the province. We boldly raised pride flags beside union flags. I was confident calling people out when they were not inclusive, and I was happy to talk with anyone who had a question about the LGBTQ community.

Another huge win for the SFL, with the help of the committee, was a court challenge to marriage commissioners who claimed that their religion allowed them to refuse to marry same-sex couples. The Saskatchewan Court of Appeal ruled that unconstitutional. The case had intervenors on both sides, from several national organizations and religions, and had national implications.

The SFL introduced its Positive Space Campaign shortly after the committee was created, based on a similar effort in Ontario. This campaign challenges the patterns of silence and marginalization that LGBTQ people experience, even in places with anti-discrimination policies. Positive space stickers displayed on office doors, union material and workplace bulletin boards helped create an environment that welcomes workplace and societal rights for LGBTQ workers. Thousands of stickers and accompanying information were distributed through the years.

In 2001, the SFL created a vice-president position on its executive council for an LGBTQ representative. This position ensured that an LGBTQ voice contributed to executive decisions and demonstrated to the labour movement that the SFL was tangibly in solidarity with the queer community.

I have been immersed in the fight for LGBTQ rights since 1997. I have been a Saskatchewan representative on the CLC Solidarity and Pride Committee since 1998, spending many years as the vice-president or alternate vice-president representing LGBTQ workers on the Canadian Labour Congress (CLC) Canadian Council. I sat as the Saskatchewan representative on the CUPE National Pink Triangle Committee for nine years and am a member of the CUPE Saskatchewan Committee Against Racism and Discrimination. I have also been president of my local for six years.

I am passionate about working to create more awareness of queer people in the community. In this regard, I have spoken to various university classes about family diversity and respecting families as they are. I love helping people understand that LGBTQ people are in our workplaces, in our communities and in our families. It is important to challenge assumptions and behaviours. Since the late 1990s, my activism has branched out to include attention to intersectionality with women, including trans women, Indigenous workers, workers of colour, workers with disabilities and most recently, to support those whose experience with domestic violence spilled over into the workplace.

THE CANADIAN HISTORICAL CONTEXT

In 1980 the CLC made a formal amendment to its constitution to include sexual orientation as a prohibited ground of discrimination. At that time, they also passed a general resolution to support gay rights and to lobby for the inclusion of sexual orientation in human rights legislation across the country. Prior to this few unions had collective-agreement language prohibiting discrimination, but after 1980 labour activists concentrated their efforts on education, collective-agreement protections and equal access to workplace benefits. With union help — both financially and politically — several court challenges and arbitration cases have been fought to achieve this goal.

The labour movement helped lead the fight for equal legal rights, including access to civil marriage rights for gay and lesbian couples. Union leaders across the country publicly voiced their support for equal marriage. Of great importance during this time was that gay and lesbian union members began to self-organize. Informal meetings, as well as activist-organized committees and working groups, started to demand formal recognition from their unions.

In 1994 CLC convention delegates overwhelmingly endorsed two policy papers: "Confronting the Mean Society" and "Sexual Orientation." The mean society paper mandated the CLC to establish four working groups for equality-seeking constituencies, one of which was the Gay, Lesbian, Bisexual Group, later renamed the Solidarity and Pride Committee, to be inclusive and to avoid the problem of having to change initials. The second policy paper denounced discrimination on the basis of sexual orientation and called on affiliated unions to bargain non-discrimination clauses. It also encouraged affiliates to develop anti-harassment policies to include sexual orientation, bargain better protection for LGBTQ workers, recognize same-sex spousal benefits, actively oppose homophobia in the workplace and unions, participate in public campaigns to win human rights for LGBTQ citizens, and prepare and distribute educational material to union members.

Many actions taken by the CLC Solidarity and Pride Committee had an educational component. One of its first projects was to survey all CLC affiliates to determine where they stood on gay, lesbian and bisexual issues with questions like: how many of your collective agreements include sexual orientation in non-discrimination clauses, and do you have a gay, lesbian, bisexual committee? The committee knew that little was actually going on, but asking the questions forced unions to do something for fear of looking less progressive than other unions. The survey helped to educate unions on their own lack of equality.

The committee undertook other educational actions or interventions at CLC conventions. One year we handed every tenth delegate a pin and brochure saying: "Congratulations — you have been selected to be gay for a day and like the rest of us your selection was entirely random. And now you are entitled to experience the following aspects of our oppression." Many who weren't selected were curious and would ask for a button, thus generating further discussion and questions.

Another educational tool we created was a booklet called "To our allies: Everything you wanted to know about lesbian, gay, bisexual and trans issues." It was distributed at conventions and conferences across the country and was used in many educational events, including some for RCMP recruits. It provided answers to questions that people might want to ask an LGBTQ community member, such as "How do lesbians get children?" It was a great tool for breaking down stereotypes. Over the years, LGBTQ activists continued to educate straight union members as well as LGBTQ members about their rights and how to enforce them. Most LGBTQ education has had this dual focus.

The CLC Solidarity and Pride Committee, as well as other union LGBTQ committees, have broadened their mandates in recent years to include combatting discrimination on the basis of gender identity and gender expression. Currently trans rights are at the forefront of this struggle. Including gender identity and gender expression in human rights codes, changing Criminal Code protections and fighting to make it easier for people to change their gender are continuous battles.

INSIDE AND OUT COURSE

In 1999 the SFL, at its Prairie School for Union Women (PSUW), offered a course called Lesbians in Unions, renamed the next year to Inside and Out, which better reflected the course content. It was developed to educate women inside the labour movement on the experience of being LGBTQ and was offered until 2009, when it was replaced with a broader human-rights course covering all equality-seeking groups.

Participants in Inside and Out had the opportunity to understand heterosexism and homophobia. In later years, it also included issues affecting the lives of transgender individuals and also Indigenous sisters who were two-spirited. Long-time facilitator Jan Cibart explained that the goal of the course was to bring awareness to the everyday challenges of workers and women who were marginalized due to their sexual orientation or gender identity. Terminology was a big part of the discussion, including how to use words like queer appropriately. Participants learned about key events in the struggle for LGBTQ rights, collective agreement language and definitions.

While the course was primarily designed to educate individuals who were straight, all participants were welcomed regardless of sexual orientation or gender identity. Many women from the LGBTQ community took the course to learn queer history and find out what their rights were in the labour movement. Disclosing one's sexual orientation or gender identity was not a prerequisite. The course's environment included humour and the chance to ask any questions without judgement, while keeping discussions respectful, safe and confidential. There were several misconceptions about the course, the biggest one being that it was only for lesbians. And facilitation was a controversial question. Did you have to be gay to teach the course? The answer was no. Was being gay a guarantee that you would facilitate the course effectively? Again, the answer was no. If you were qualified to be a facilitator and you were from the LGBTQ community, you would bring to the course a different umbrella of experiences.

The course made a positive impact. Jan recalled participants saying that Inside and Out was not their first choice to take but, by the end, they were grateful that they had learned so much. Sometimes they felt comfortable and safe enough to open up about their own sexuality or that of someone close to them. Because of the course structure, participants had deep conversations about marginalization and other women's issues. Participants always appreciated the personal stories and experiences of LGBTQ facilitators and other participants, so much so that it was hard to cover the course content in the available time. Participants loved to ask questions such as: What happened when you came out? Who was supportive? Who wasn't? What was it like for your children?

During the first hours of the course, some participants would say, "Well, I'm not homophobic but …" or "I don't dislike gay people but …" It was rewarding as a facilitator to see them evolve through their fears and misunderstandings to a place where they could embrace their new knowledge and head in a more positive direction.

PSUW AND LGBTQ

The Prairie School for Union Women was created to advance women's equality and leadership inside the labour movement, but most of the women involved in the organizing were straight white women. Every year there was an appeal to PSUW participants to join the Steering Committee. This effort has not been successful, however, and more work is needed to ensure fuller representation. Course designers and facilitators are required to apply an equality lens to all courses, as well as generally throughout the school, but more focused effort is required.

By offering courses focusing on LGBTQ issues and generally including LGBTQ women in the PSUW discourse from the school's beginning, the PSUW helped union women become more accepting of the relationships of LGBTQ couples and equating them to heterosexual relationships. The more women have a chance to talk and interact with LGBTQ participants and staff, the more educated and supportive they become. The school wasn't the first place in the SFL where people were out, but it was the first place women were safe and celebrated being out. Openly lesbian women worked at the PSUW and engaged in various ways during the school, and that was okay.

However, some school participants were not all right with lesbians. Some anti-gay sentiments were pretty entrenched, as demonstrated by overheard comments like: "PSUW was where all the dykes went to find each other." The existence of the school and its focus on diversity alarmed some and brought latent bigotry out in the open. Some women participants felt they would be targeted by their co-workers or other participants because they were taking Inside and Out and complained if they were placed in the course when their first or second choices weren't available. Fortunately, after some encouragement, most were happy and comfortable with the information — a real liberation!

I remember a couple of quite vocal and outrageous lesbians who pushed boundaries to get reactions. They would tease straight women and offer them toaster ovens (a not-so-secret reward for coming out, thanks to Ellen DeGeneres's television show). Pushing women's comfort levels with humour helped to ease some of the stress around gay issues and open up further discussion. A straight woman shared with me her empathy and a new understanding of how a lesbian might feel being on the other end of the teasing. She acknowledged that the feeling of discomfort could cut both ways.

For education within the LGBTQ community, the PSUW has been instrumental in two ways: lesbians feel comfortable being out at a union function and straight women feel comfortable having an open discussion about "gayness." This has been an important phenomenon for both communities. It created a critical mass: the point at which enough people having the discussion made it possible for even more people to have those discussions.

Like other union schools and conferences, the PSUW makes a clear anti-harassment statement during its opening plenary. Some people question why this is necessary at women-only labour education. The reality is that there can still be plenty of harassment: racist, homophobic, transphobic, even sexist comments. The school distributes and displays other educational messages about equality, including equality posters, stickers, allies' booklets, movie nights with equality themed movies such as *Pride, Freehold* or *Made in Dagenham*. These plant seeds of equality and become part of the PSUW culture.

Another extremely important contribution of the PSUW to LGBTQ lives is the childcare offered at the school. By welcoming children from diverse families, the school helps children define their own social norms and challenges them to move beyond the limitations society tries to create. The PSUW also gives courage to organizers of other SFL educational events to think beyond the standard course options and start offering more equality courses. It leads them to challenge course facilitators to put an equality lens on courses they may have presented the same way for years.

CONCLUSION

My transformation to the activist I am today is grounded in women-only labour education. Working in a safe and mostly respectful environment allowed me to find my voice. I have gained the confidence to become a leader and a spokesperson for human rights and continue to be a social justice activist. At times I have felt brave and at times I have felt broken, but because of my experiences and education I am able to confront limits and push boundaries.

Educating one leads to the education of others. My education through the labour movement has changed my life, and I have changed others' lives by helping them understand issues from a queer perspective. Our committee members and I have spoken about LGBTQ issues to labour organizations, trade union members, university students, RCMP recruits, the media and other organizations. We have shared stories, experiences, stickers, letters, booklets and whatever else we can to ensure the information is accessible.

Challenging my own union and the labour movement in general to choose more diverse, representative leaders has become a passion. Although there are few lesbian or trans women in union leadership positions, the practical work that needs to get done is occurring, and we are slowly seeing that our sexual orientation is a non-issue. Backlash still occurs, and religion often interferes. But there is hope. Labour people understand that "an injury to one is an injury to all." We understand the fragility of all rights and know we need to stand together when we are fighting for our rights and the rights of others.

CHAPTER FIVE

THE WALL
Reflections on a Workshop Methodology

Bev Burke and Suzanne Doerge

In a one-day workshop, we created a beautiful wall that looked like a piece of art. We posted differently coloured stones speaking about the pain, fatigue and anger women are feeling with the changes in the economy. But it wasn't depressing because we realized the strength we have as women to change it. There were all of those paper women running all over it, identifying actions we can take to support each other — and to challenge privatization and globalization.
— workshop participant, CUPE Women's Conference 1998

In this chapter we, the creators and facilitators of The Wall methodology, give readers an overview of the thinking behind the methodology — what it is and where the idea came from.[1] We take you for a walk along the wall so that you can become familiar with the graphics that are used and the types of discussion that emerge. More importantly, however, we share our experiences of what this methodology can achieve for union women and some of the challenges we have faced as facilitators in using it. We also discuss how The Wall has been used both in Canada and internationally and some of the many ways women have adapted the methodology to meet and resolve local needs and issues.

WHAT IS THE WALL WORKSHOP?

This visual, participatory workshop uses the image of a stone wall to explore ways in which globalization has taken advantage of women and to discover opportunities for change. Across Canada and internationally, The Wall has been used as a tool to enable women, whether they are rank and file, researchers or union leaders, to visibly see the impact of neoliberal policies and strategize together. From the Movement of Women Workers in Nicaragua (MEC) to public-sector workers in Canada and around the world,

Woman working with The Wall, p. 14 from English Guide

this participatory tool has provided a way for women to name their personal experiences and link them to the macro-economy.

Women often do not think they know anything about the economy. Therefore, we chose a visual, participatory method, which supports learning for many women, and started with sharing our everyday experiences. We found few other examples of addressing economic issues using this kind of methodology. We chose the stone wall to represent the economy, which is made up of interrelated parts that build upon one another. The stones at the top of the metaphoric wall represent the ways that we, as women, are being affected in our daily lives by changes in the economy — at home, in the community, in the workplace and in our unions. This is often the only part of the wall that we see. To better understand our experiences, we need to explore the bottom of the wall to look at how women's work is changing and why. We look at the gains we have made to promote equality and the changes that need to take place today so that women's work is valued and respected. The plants at the very bottom of the wall represent signs of hope, initiatives currently underway that can grow up this wall and transform it.

Here is what it looks like before we begin.

And here is The Wall at the end of the day!

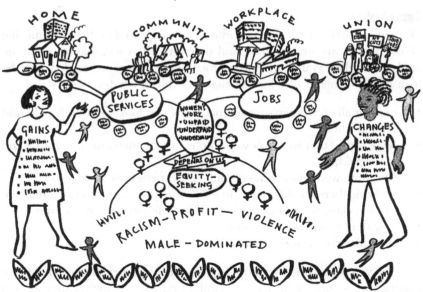

WHERE DID THE WALL COME FROM?

Suzanne Doerge developed the concept of The Wall methodology for a 1993 national conference sponsored by the Task Force on the Feminine Face of Poverty. In 1998, Suzanne and Bev Burke developed the workshop further for the Canadian Union of Public Employees' (CUPE's) Fifth National Women's Conference. Interest from unions across the country and internationally led to the publication of a facilitator's guide in 2000, at the time of the World March of Women, called "Starting with Women's Lives: Changing Today's Economy." The Public Service Alliance of Canada (PSAC) translated the original guide into French. Upon piloting the workshop in Nicaragua with the women's organization Puntos de Encuentro, Oxfam Canada funded the development of a Latin American adaptation, in Spanish, co-authored by Suzanne Doerge and Fernández Piñon in 2004. In 2005, the English guide was updated and enhanced. The guide is currently available in English, French and Spanish and can be downloaded for free from The Wall website www.wallworkshop.com.

THE THINKING BEHIND THE WALL METHODOLOGY

The Wall draws upon two bodies of knowledge: gender analysis and popular education, and, in particular, feminist popular education. We briefly take a look at each of these bodies of knowledge and why we think they are important to The Wall.

Gender Analysis

Women's experiences and contributions, although vital in the economic life of our world, are undervalued and therefore often invisible in economic analyses. In The Wall workshop, women's experiences are made visible by focusing on elements of a gender analysis, which includes:

- making all of women's experience visible by looking at both paid and unpaid work;
- recognizing that women's work tends to be undervalued, invisible and underpaid;
- exploring women's and men's different experiences at work;
- realizing there are differences in power and privilege among women due to race, class, sexual orientation, ability, religion, age and country;
- affirming women's power; and
- strengthening women's leadership.

A key step is to begin with our experiences as women and to share those experiences to find patterns and similarities. Due to inequalities among women, such as related to age, class, race and sexual orientation, we recognize our differences. We look at the differences between men's and women's work experiences, both in paid work done in workplaces and in unpaid work done at home and in the community. We examine the structures, policies and programs that perpetuate these inequalities and formulate actions we can take to challenge them.

Part way through each workshop we pose the following question to workshop participants: "What would happen tomorrow if we women withdrew our labour?" This question helps women begin to think about all the unpaid work they do at home and in the community, as well as the kinds of paid jobs that many women have, such as clerical or administrative work, which tends to keep organizations running. Thinking about women's collective contributions to the economy helps workshop participants come to understand that the entire economy is dependent upon the work that women do. The ways in which the elements of a gender analysis are woven in The Wall workshops are discussed in more detail later in the chapter.

Popular Education

While gender analysis affects how we look at the content of The Wall workshops, popular education affects how we look at the process — the education methodology we use. Brazilian educator Paulo Freire (1970) originally developed the idea of popular education. In Spanish *popular* means by, for, and of the people. The goal of popular education is to challenge existing power relations and to support struggles for social change that benefits the majority, not just a few. Popular education takes sides — it does not pretend to be neutral. So, it is no surprise that this methodology has been widely used in the labour movement, including here in Canada. Some key principles of popular education include:

- Value and respect for the experience of workers — in this case particularly the experience of women workers;
- Model and develop democratic practices. There is a participatory approach to building the analysis where teachers and students learn together;
- Encourage equitable participation and challenge inequities;
- Draw on the whole person; and
- Encourage collective action for change.

The Wall workshops utilize the spiral as follows: 1) women begin by sharing experiences of changes in jobs and public services; 2) the group identifies differences and similarities in their experience; 3) an experience is analyzed and new information and theory shared (how are women affected differently from one another and from men; who benefits from the current economic model; is there a link to globalization); and 4) the workshop moves

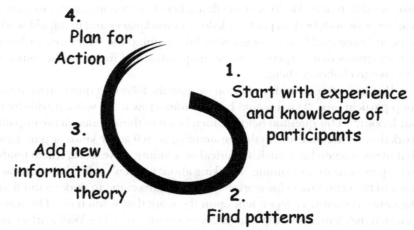

The spiral illustrates the key moments in the methodology of popular education
Source: Burke, Geronimo, Martin, Thomas and Wall 2002: 57.

to action: signs of hope for the future and actions women are taking or can take together.

Feminist Popular Education

While the principles of feminist popular education are similar to those of popular education, there are a few areas that we have found to be particularly important. Feminist popular education places a good deal of emphasis on drawing on the whole person — heart, mind, body and spirit. As women build an analysis together and can see visually how their experiences are related to those of other women and to the broader issues, they also build confidence. During The Wall workshops there are also exercises which use and help us get more in touch with our bodies. These are not add-ons, but rather are an important part of doing the analysis.

A WALK ALONG THE WALL

Naming the Changes

Let us go for a walk along the wall and explore its different parts and how they get developed by the participants. We begin by asking women to name ways that social services and jobs have been changing over the past ten years. In pairs, participants write key changes on coloured stones and post them on the wall. After all the stones have been posted facilitators review two or three relevant statistics on cards posted on the side of the wall.

Next, we look at how these changes to jobs and social services are affecting women's lives. Participants are divided into four groups: home, community,

workplace and union. The members of each group share the impact of the changes on their lives in that particular area. These experiences are summarized on coloured paper stones and posted in the relevant area on the top of the wall. After all the groups have posted, participants identify patterns and draw lines to show connections. Stress and violence are threads that usually run through the four areas.

The Work Women Do

This is a chance to have some fun while learning about the nature of women's work in the global economy. Participants are introduced to the term *triple role*, which refers to the multiple roles that women play in their homes, communities and workplaces; and for the activist in the union, it is the quadruple role! Small groups are given a scenario in which a woman is

---

A sample scenario is "Baby's Burping"
As you had an important meeting at work today, you wore your new blouse.
After picking up your baby at daycare, you went straight to a parents' meeting to discuss cuts to education. You are raising your hand to make an important point, when your baby burps on your new blouse, and you know you had better wipe it off immediately. You find yourself: Juggling your baby, trying to wipe off the stain, while keeping your hand in the air to make your point.

---

doing three things at once. Each group prepares and presents the scenario to the others, using mime.

The scenario presentations lead to a discussion about the amount of work that women do and how it is often unpaid, underpaid and undervalued. The facilitator shares some key statistics about both the unpaid and underpaid work that women do. She then places a purple stone in the centre of the wall with the caption, "Women's Work: Unpaid, Underpaid, Undervalued," and points out that the current global economy depends upon this in order to function. Participants then identify the gains women have made toward achieving equality and having their labour valued. Ideas are written on one of the large woman figures on the wall.

How We Are Affected Differently

After dividing into four small groups, the participants in two groups discuss ways in which women are affected differently than men by these changes in jobs and social services. Ideas are written on purple women-symbol-shaped stones. The other two groups discuss how women in equity-seeking groups (single mothers, young or older women, women of colour, recent immigrants, women in poverty, etc.) are affected by these changes. In plenary, everyone shares and posts their stones. The facilitator helps the groups draw connections.

Why Is This Happening?

Small groups discuss why this is happening and write their ideas on gold-coloured stones, which are then posted on the wall. The facilitator helps participants draw connections and identify key ideas. Key ideas are written on the wall, and fact sheets on aspects of globalization are distributed. Looking at the entire wall, the facilitator asks participants how this makes them feel. Often, the response is "overwhelmed!"

Naming Our Power and Our Allies

Each woman is given a card with the name of an individual or institution on it. All the participants are asked to line up across the room according to how much power the person or organization on her card has and how much the person or organization benefits from the wall. Discussion follows in the line-up about who benefits the most and the least, what power the different women in the line have to change the wall, and where their power comes from.

The facilitator reviews the three kinds of power: 1) *power-over*, where one person or group has power over another person or group, e.g., racism, sexism; 2) *power-within*, which comes from inner strength, self-confidence, sense of determination, spiritual source; and 3) *power-with*, otherwise expressed as solidarity, sisterhood, community. We increase our power when we join with others (Starhawk 1989).

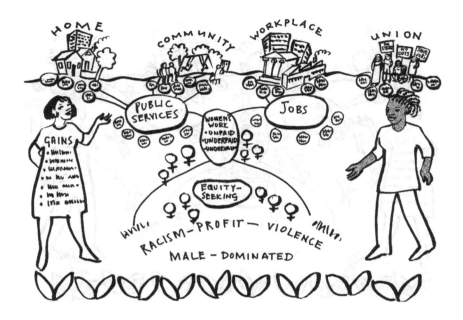

The group is then asked to identify allies in the line-up and to link arms with them. Finally, after everyone has returned to their seats, the facilitator asks what would happen to the wall if we, as women, were to withdraw our paid and our unpaid labour tomorrow. People call out answers and the facilitator posts a paper crack (a jagged piece of paper cut in the shape of a crack titled *DEPENDS ON US*) in a central location on the wall, noting that the fact that the economy's dependence on women is a key source of our power to change it.

We end by asking the group, "Who's got the power?" which evolves into a chant, "Who's got the power? We've got the power!"

Moving to Action

The facilitator explains that the leaves at the bottom of the wall represent signs of hope that have the potential to grow up the wall and transform it. Participants are asked to identify actions already underway in the unions and elsewhere that are signs of hope and to write them on the leaves. The group then brainstorms changes needed to challenge the wall, and these ideas are listed on the woman on the right side of the wall.

Small groups then form to identify concrete actions that union women can take. These ideas are written on bright pink women figures. The ideas are shared and posted on the part of the wall their action challenges or supports. Depending on the group, we then discuss next steps, such as a joint action and individual actions back in the local union or workplace.

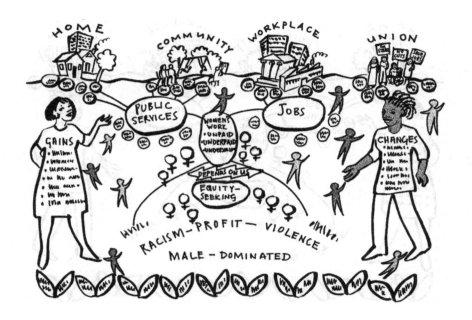

WHAT THE WALL ACHIEVES FOR UNION WOMEN

With the exception of Nicaragua, we have limited long-term evaluation data to identify what women have done as a result of The Wall workshops. However, we can identify the following impacts from participant evaluations and feedback we have received.

Women No Longer Feel Alone

"It isn't just me!" In The Wall process, women begin to discover that other women are having many of the same difficulties as they face with social program cuts, work piling up at home and taking care of both children and elders. One participant came up after a workshop in tears and said, "I finally understand that it is not that there's something wrong with me. I have a hell of a lot on my plate!"

Women Link Union/Workplace Experiences with Community/Home

The Wall allows the analysis to draw on all aspects of women's lives. In particular, the link between women's union and workplace experiences and their communities and homes highlights the issue of women's unpaid work at home and in the community as well as workplace issues. At a moment when there are increased attempts to build alliances between labour and other sectors of the popular movement, this link is particularly important and also points to a critical role for union women in building these alliances.

Women Share What They've Learned with Sisters

Key results from the evaluation of the program in Nicaragua also showed that women shared what they had learned with their sisters and became aware of their collective contribution to both the domestic and national economies. (See the box on MEC in Nicaragua.)

Women Draw On Their Hearts, Bodies, Minds and Spirits

Typically, in education, we focus on the mind and on transmitting facts and information. Without a simultaneous focus on our hearts, bodies and spirit we will not necessarily experience a change in awareness or consciousness on a deep level. By remaining in our heads, the change is not very profound. But if the learning touches us more deeply — if people are moved to laughter, tears and "ah- hah" moments — it leaves a stronger memory and is more likely to bring about sustainable change. Making learning visual — using the wall drawing and having women build their analyses together — also leaves a much longer lasting memory of the process. In many cases women take their wall back with them to their union or workplace (if permitted).

Women Relate the Economy to Their Lives

One of the exciting things about The Wall method of analysis is that it builds confidence in women to be able to talk about economic issues. The top of the wall is the key part of this approach to raising women's awareness. Nurses, for example, name the changes to the nursing profession and in health-care provision. In small groups, they share stories about how each of them experiences these changes in their own homes, communities, workplaces, unions and associations. There are similar stories of women feeling stressed and stretched as they are asked to do more and more. They talk about the impacts on family life and of increased violence and backlash against the gains women have made around pay equity, affirmative action and union support. Later they are able to link what women experience in their daily lives with things that are happening at a national or global level. One participant said:

> So when I go back to my daily life and I'm running around like crazy in great big shopping stores, or when I am expected to volunteer here and there because of cutbacks in education, then there's a light that goes on that says: This isn't just me! This is symptomatic of a larger systemic something that's happening!

Women Feel Increased Sense of Empowerment

There is a moment in The Wall workshop when we've finished the analysis and women are feeling overwhelmed. That is when we do the power line-up — not only to talk about power, but also to get people up on their feet, shifting their bodies from being passive in their seats to being up and active. It helps to create that mental shift from "I'm oppressed by the corporations and there's no way in the world we can do anything" to "Yes, there's something we can do!" The power line-up shows that we do have power and when we link with other women, our allies, we can increase that power to make change.

Women Contribute Different Ways of Learning

Early in the analysis, we look at who is most affected by the changes to jobs and social programs. The process honours different ways of learning by allowing women to speak from their own experience. For some, this is their own lived experience. Others, those from a research background for example, are able to add their knowledge without lecturing. Both ways of knowing are equally valued.

Women Build Leadership Skills

The Wall was used specifically in Colombia by the Colombian Workers Central (CUT) in a workshop to build women trade union leadership. (See the section on Adaptations). The Wall includes a discussion on actions we can take, which gives women strategies to draw on when they return to their unions. Other impacts mentioned above, increased confidence in being able to talk about the economy, not feeling alone and feeling more empowered are all contributions to building women union leaders.

CHALLENGES

Women Feel Overwhelmed

The visual of the wall, which women build together, illustrates what we, as women, face in the economy and how the structure of the global economy affects our daily lives. This can be overwhelming, so we have built in ways to counter this by:

- writing on the wall the gains that women and unions have made;
- doing a power line-up to identify our allies and the power we have as women; and
- posting the large crack in the centre of the wall to show how the wall depends on women and so gives women some power to change it.

The reality of the system we face, however, is still there, and women are affected by the visual of that power.

Preparing the Materials

Union women educators are busy people. After the first publication of the facilitator's guide, we received feedback about the amount of preparation required by the facilitators for this visual methodology. There are a lot of props required! We tried to address this problem in the second edition of the guide by including templates of the various props required that can simply be photocopied. However, there is still a lot of preparation work to do for The Wall workshops.

Sharing in a Mixed-Gender Space

In the early stages of the evolution of The Wall we bumped into problems when we worked with a mixed group of men and women. We found it significantly affected how the women participated. For example, when there were just a couple of men in the room, some women tended to try to support and nurture them, so they would not feel left out. Other women, particularly those who had suffered any kind of violence, had a lot of difficulty talking easily with men in the room. Still other women tended to habitually defer to men. Our conclusion: the tool works best when it is a women-only space.

As this is not always possible, we designed a different process of economic analysis to use in the few workshops where men are present, such as the Canadian Labour Congress (CLC) workshop on privatization, Vibrant Communities workshop on gender and poverty reduction, and some of the Canadian Nursing Association (CNA) workshops that we will look at later. Initially, we had men looking at the experiences of women they know, and we found this was not effective. Consequently, the different economic analysis designed for workshops where men are present to help men to look at and consider their own experiences.

ADAPTING FROM THE GLOBAL NORTH TO THE GLOBAL SOUTH

Through the women's department at the CLC, we were invited by Public Service International (PSI) to work with The Wall at their Inter-American regional women's conference in Panama in October 2000 with women leaders from fifteen countries across the Americas. We were nervous! We did not know if The Wall would be relevant to women in Latin America. We decided to bring a list of the changes to jobs and social programs identified by Canadian public sector union women as a way to begin the workshop. We were astounded when we discovered that, with just a few exceptions, the trends were the same, but deeper, for women in developing countries. We were then invited by the PSI to facilitate The Wall at regional women's conferences in Asia and Africa, and we feared the same thing. Was it possible that the methodology and analysis could work in such different contexts?

We took with us the list of changes to jobs and social programs that we used in Panama. In Africa, there were clear differences, such as the impact of AIDS on all areas of women's lives, including union leadership and deeper poverty. However, the trends were much the same. Changes to services included cuts, privatization, increasing cost of water and electricity. Changes to jobs involved loss of union jobs, more job insecurity, more informal work and increased workload, to name a few. And we had the same experience in Asia. We do not want to minimize the differences across countries, but from the international workshops, we learned that the trends in globalization are strikingly similar.

Working Across Languages and Cultures

As mentioned above, The Wall was used in PSI women's conferences in three regions: Americas (2000), Asia (2001) and Africa (2003). Some of this work was challenging. For example, at the regional conference in South Korea, we were happy to be facilitating with two Japanese sisters. A day before the workshop was to begin, however, we discovered they did not speak any English, and indeed we did not speak Japanese. Additionally, the workshop proceedings were being translated, in the room, into many other languages. We decided to organize sub-groups whose members worked in their common language, with translation needed in a few groups. In plenary, the sub-groups posted on the wall in their own language, with excellent simultaneous translation into all the languages spoken in the room. And to our surprise, this way of doing it was highly successful.

Accumulating all these experiences for the PSI Congress held in Ottawa in 2002, a wall display was developed, including a guidebook (Public Service International) to the display, which walked people through The Wall. The guidebook was written in the original languages of The Wall — English, French, and Spanish — and was also translated into additional languages, including Japanese and Swedish. As follow-up to their work with PSI, several Japanese unions used The Wall, including the All Japan Prefectural and Municipal Workers Union, which held a workshop for union leaders using a Japanese translation of the guide. They reported: "Our discussion was shaped into the wall and the analysis made the Japanese economy, systems and laws easier to understand and opened up realistic approaches we can actually take."

WHO HAS USED THE WALL AND HOW?

The Wall has been used both in Canada and internationally primarily with union women, both public and private sector, the Canadian Nurses Association (CNA) and several community groups focusing primarily on gender and poverty. To date we are aware of more than twenty-five unions who have used and adapted The Wall in Canada and around the world (See also The Wall website at www.wallworkshop.com for more detailed accounts and photos from many of the workshops mentioned in this section.) Some of the most common uses have been in public sector women's conferences and courses to explore issues such as the impacts on diverse union women of increasing workload and changes/cuts to jobs and social services. The CLC adapted The Wall to use in an Indigenous workers and workers of colour conference on social and economic transformation in 2002 and in a national conference on privatization in 2001. In this latter adaptation, the wall began with four centre stones: Jobs, Social Services, Privatization and Deregulation. One delegate to that conference said: "Building the wall made us think about how to tear down the privatization wall!"

Below are some other examples of how The Wall has been used, followed by further adaptations for other specific themes and issues.

The Wall in Spanish — La Pared

Suzanne Doerge and Montserrat Fernández Piñon, a Spanish educator working in Nicaragua, worked with a women's organization in Nicaragua, Puntos de Encuentro, to adapt and pilot the methodology for the Nicaraguan context. In the Canadian version, the workshop begins with changes to jobs and public services, while in the Nicaraguan context it was recognized that, given the state of the economy, many women would never hold a formal job or have access to public services. Therefore, the Nicaraguan workshop began with three key stones: Ways We Earn a Living, Public Services for those who had access to them and Cost of Living, which touched all the participants. It was discovered that the workshop worked well with women with limited literacy and a wide range of economic and life situations (such as *maquila* workers, agricultural workers, nurses). Thanks to support from the Steelworkers Humanity Fund, CUSO and Oxfam Canada, a Spanish facilitator's guide was produced in 2004. In 2006, a workshop was held to train twenty-eight facilitators from five Central American countries representing fifteen organizations. Another workshop, sponsored by Sector Mujer with funds from Oxfam Canada, was held in Guatemala, primarily with Indigenous women leaders.

Economic Literacy for Maquila Workers in Nicaragua: MEC

The assumption in Nicaragua, as in many other countries, is that economics are "for men" and that women contribute little to the economy. As a result, a course in economic literacy for women from a gender perspective, and especially for women workers and women living in poverty, was groundbreaking. El Movimiento Maria Elena Cuadra (MEC) is the largest women's organization in Nicaragua, the majority being *maquila* workers in the free-trade zones. It trained 3,000 women in the first three years of the program. The Wall methodology showed how larger issues like globalization and international trade linked to women's daily lives and made visible women's contribution to the economy. Key results from the evaluation of the program included increased self-esteem and empowerment of women, both individually and collectively. Participants were also committed to share what they learned with others.

Source: CAWN 2008.

A major user of the Spanish guide has been MEC, the Movement of Women Workers and Unemployed Women, or El Movimiento Maria Elena Cuadra, which works with women in the sweatshop sector to help them develop economic literacy skills to understand the causes of their working conditions and how to change them. A major evaluation was completed in 2008 (see Box).

Other International Uses

In Denmark in 2001, the CNA brought together nursing association partners from eight countries (South Africa, Ethiopia, Indonesia, Vietnam, Kosovo, El Salvador, Nicaragua, Ecuador and Canada) to participate in a Wall workshop to identify common trends in health care and nursing. In 2002, nurses from across Vietnam used The Wall to inform their national nursing strategy at a time when they were opening up to globalization and starting to privatize. In El Salvador, The Wall was used as part of a strategy to help nurses develop analytical skills to be able to enter into negotiations with the government on modernization of health care.

A bilingual Wall workshop (English and Spanish) was held at the 2005 Association for Women's Rights in Development conference in Thailand, where women from many countries participated. It was also used in a workshop in Venezuela as part of the World Social Forum in 2006. The Solidarity Center for the American Federation of Labor (AFL-CIO) in Mexico has also used The Wall in their gender program with their Mexican partners. In Pittsburg in 2001, over 600 Steelworkers from the U.S. and Canada used The Wall at their Sisters in Solidarity Conference. Examples of what participants said they were taking back to their workplaces and local unions include: "A stronger, more confident voice to speak up"; "I will encourage and support younger workers"; "I am going to help visible minority women to get more involved in the union"; "help to get child care in the workplace by running for the negotiating committee"; and "help the union work in coalition with community groups."

THE WALL ADAPTATIONS

The Wall has taken on a life of its own. We have heard stories about women facilitating Wall workshops in many places, including Kosovo, Japan, Colombia, Middle Eastern countries and Greenland. It is important to stress that this tool now really belongs to a lot of people. We are sure that many people have made adaptations we are not aware of. We think the fact that women in Canada and around the world have been picking up and claiming the method for their own is a fitting journey for a method of analysis created to empower women. That said, we do want to highlight a few adaptations which others might find especially useful. We suggest you also refer to uses by unions and others described throughout the text for more ideas.

Leadership Training of Trade Union Activists

Following the PSI women's conference in Panama, The Wall was adapted by the Colombian Workers Central (CUT) in Colombia for a five-day national leadership course in August 2000 for women trade union activists to analyze their national context (marked by conflict, the impact of structural adjustment and a crisis in the unions) and to seek alternatives. The workshop also aimed to develop a strategy to increase the number of women in leadership and get the specific demands of women workers into the political platform of the union. Instead of starting with jobs and social programs, they began with four main stones labeled as follows: Crisis of Governance, Neoliberal Economic Model, Armed Conflict and the Role of Social Organizations. In the centre, they added a drawing of a woman's uterus on which they wrote the kinds of invisible work that women do. The organizers commented: "La Pared (The Wall) is a valuable educational tool that makes it possible to transcend the analysis of academics as it draws from the day-to-day experience of women workers."

Violence Against Women

The Canadian Autoworkers Union (now Unifor) women's conference in 2006 was attended by about 175 women, with day one spent in The Wall workshops. The top of the wall recorded the visible costs of violence that came out of the discussions and looked at those costs in the various parts of women's lives — and in the broader national and global world.

The middle of the wall holds up the top. Here we recorded factors that support violence and allow it to continue, and these are often not visible. We looked at three areas. First was economic inequality and how women's work is structured, by using a mime exercise and discussion of women's work from the facilitator's guide. Second was the role of government policies, for which we adapted the power line-up from the guide, so women lined up according to how vulnerable they are to violence. Then we introduced various government policies on housing, education and other supports and had women move along the line if that policy made them more or less vulnerable to violence. Third, we looked at how media messages and images of women support violence, using an edited version of the film *The Strength to Resist* (Cambridge Documentary Films 2001).

The bottom of the wall used the plants in the original guide to record actions already taken to end violence against women. Women then planned actions to take back to their locals and communities. These were posted on the women action figures from the original wall. In addition to group actions, participants recorded on the drawing of women action figures an individual action they wished to take when they got home. As in the original version, the two women on the wall were used to record gains made in the elimination of violence and to record the challenges we still face.

An additional piece, built into the second day of the workshop, involved introducing some tools and skills for action prior to asking women to develop action plans. These included exercises in understanding how the union works, thinking outside the box (creative actions) and lobbying or speaking about violence.

Nursing and Health Care

The Wall workshops sponsored by the CNA brought together nurses and other health professionals in Canada and many other countries to explore the impact of globalization on the profession. The workshops began with the image of a globe and figures walking across it to ask what is contributing to the migration of nurses around the globe. Then the workshop participants began creating the wall starting with two main stones: Nursing and Health Systems, identifying the changes and their impact on their lives. The triple-role exercise and a mime activity helped them to discover the ways in which the devaluing of women's work leads to the devaluing and underfunding of nursing. Nurses in El Salvador, Vietnam, Ethiopia and Indonesia all had similar stories to tell and used The Wall to strategize on how they could turn this around.

Human Rights

The Canadian Union of Postal Workers (CUPW) Human Rights Forum in 2004 was attended by about a hundred members from the four equity groups that make up the CUPW Human Rights Committee: workers of colour, Indigenous workers, differently abled workers, LGBTQ workers. Participants began The Wall discussion in equity caucus workshops, where they were asked to name how discrimination happens for them. Then in mixed equity groups, they began to build the wall, starting with one main stone in the centre for each equity group. Each equity group posted their experiences of discrimination on small stones around their corresponding large stone and talked about the impact of discrimination in the home, community, workplace and union. The full group discussed similarities and differences across the four equity groups, (naming gender, class and age) and named the foundation stones of discrimination and oppression. Facilitators used the "naming our power" exercise to talk about both power and privilege to identify the gains we have made, the signs of hope and the strengths we bring to meet the challenges, and then talked about working with allies. Finally, in regional caucuses, participants developed action plans to push the equity agenda forward in their unions and in their communities.

CONCLUSION

The Wall methodology continues to be relevant in today's economy. In fact, at a time when gains made by women and unions are being rolled back, The Wall can be a valuable tool in understanding the context and possible ways to create change. We thank the hundreds of participants and facilitators in the many workshop experiences described above — and in many other experiences we do not know about! Without all the energy and enthusiasm of so many women in so many unions and social movement organizations, in so many different parts of Canada and around the world, none of this would have been possible. As we begin The Wall with women's experiences, let us end the chapter with what women have said about their experiences in the workshops:

> I feel re-energized, motivated and ready to take on the battle against privatization!

> *Yo no sabia nada y era muy timida. Aprendi a valorarme a mi misma y a sentirme igual a los demas.* [I did not know anything and was very timid. I learned to value myself and to feel equal to others].

> *Hemos aprendido a defendernos, para no ser aplastadas como cucarachas!* (We learned how to defend ourselves so as not to be squashed like cockroaches).

> I have the capacity to effect change and be an asset to the movement.... Women can make a difference. The first step is ours!

> We can see more clearly where the power lies to address inequality and the potential to address inequities when working together inside and outside of the union in coalition.

> So, who's got the power? We've got the power!

Note

1. Suzanne and Bev wish to acknowledge and thank Margie Adam from Artwork for the wonderful wall graphics; Montserrat Fernández Piñon, who co-authored the Spanish guide with support from Puntos de Encuentro in Nicaragua and Oxfam Canada; and the in-kind and financial support from Canadian unions, in particular CAW, CLC, CUPE, CUPW, OPSEU, PSAC and USW.

CHAPTER SIX

REGINA V. POLK WOMEN'S LABOR LEADERSHIP CONFERENCE
Whole Body, Whole-life Struggle

Helena Worthen

For eleven years, between 2000 and 2011, I ran the annual Regina V. Polk Women's Labor Leadership Conference out of the University of Illinois Labor Education Program. It feels strange to say, "I ran" the conference. In labour education, people rarely say, "*I*" did something. We say, "*We*" did this or that. Especially in women's labour education, work is collective. Because of the way Polk is funded, however, whoever runs Polk has a free hand to design the agenda, create the curriculum and do the staffing and recruiting. She also takes responsibility for what happens, for better or worse.

These factors made Polk different from the annual women's summer schools run by the United Association for Labor Education (UALE), which are a shared project with women trade unionists and faculty at other regional colleges or universities (Shaughnessey and Hamilton 2015). So, although many great women taught at Polk, participated in it, refined the curriculum and led the workshops, Polk was really mine to work with, for better or worse. Now, Emily LaBarbera Twarog, my successor at the University of Illinois, can say, "I run the Polk Conference." And she's doing a wonderful job.

Polk's funding came from the Regina Polk Fund for Women's Labor Leadership. It generously covered housing, plentiful food, entertainment and some honoraria for instructors. It allowed most of the women participants to come on full scholarships and also made it possible to support and even pay past participants who were invited back as coaches. While a few of the Polk participants had good-paying jobs and were accustomed to nice accommodations, many others worked low-wage jobs, so staying in a hotel for four days was a rare pleasure. The money was awarded annually following presentations of proposals at a lunch hosted by the chair of the fund, Tom Heagy.

I got a "free hand" running Polk because, between 2001 and 2007, I was the only woman in the Illinois Labor Education Program. Being a woman mattered because even then, in the first decade of the twenty-first century, labour education was, at least in the U.S., still a man's world. "Labour" was macho, "workers" meant male factory workers, and the whole field of employment relations aspired to be a social science based on hard quantitative research. If a woman was hired at all, she was likely to be assigned sexual harassment classes and assertiveness training courses, topics deemed appropriate to what was then a newly organized white-collar, female demographic. Men, by contrast, would teach contract bargaining.

To help at Polk, I relied heavily on two of the best women labour educators I knew: Judy Ancel, from the University of Missouri Kansas City, and Ruth Needleman, from the University of Indiana in Gary. Also, Anne Feeney, a singer, performer, labour lawyer and activist, would join us for the entire four days of each conference. She played a role that was partly musician, partly teacher, but also articulate witness to most of the big labour fights of the last forty years in the U.S.

So, what do you do, when you have enough money, good friends to work with and a free hand to organize things the way you want? Let us begin with the story of where the "enough money" came from.

WHO WAS REGINA V. POLK?

Regina V. Polk, for whom the conference is named, worked for Teamsters 743, one of the biggest unions in Chicago. She was killed on the job in 1984 when she was thirty-three years old. "Killed on the job" is both accurate and misleading: she died in a plane crash going from Chicago south to Carbondale for a meeting about job training. But when you read the story of her life, you cannot help wonder at the ways Gina, as people called her, was pushing the limits.

Everything I know about Gina comes from two sources. First, there were a few people who actually knew her and would come and talk about her at the Polk conference. Twenty years after her death, these people, men and women alike, would weep tears when they talked about her. The second source is her 2008 biography, *I Am a Teamster*, by Terry Spencer Hesser. Commissioned by the Regina Polk Fund for Labor Leadership, the book is well researched and well written. It shows readers a smart, focused, assertive young woman with an easily ignited temper and a passion for expensive clothes. The photographs in Hesser's book reveal a woman with a face like Ingrid Bergman's. She seems to have led a bit of a hippie life in California before moving east to go to the University of Chicago.

The International Brotherhood of Teamsters (IBT) first hired Gina part-time after she got fired for trying to organize fellow workers at a north-side restaurant. She rose in the union from part-time help to an organizer to business agent; she became eligible to run for office, which may have made her seem like a threat to someone.

Hesser describes her as a truly gifted unionist. In a grievance hearing, she would demonstrate a steel-trap grasp of the contract. On a picket line, she was capable of slapping a police officer who insulted her. Winning two major organizing campaigns among white-collar workers, mostly women, raised her profile in the union. She was invited to give a speech at the annual stewards' training banquet. She prepared intensively by listening to a speech given by Jimmy Hoffa in the 1960s and wrote a powerful piece of classic motivational union rhetoric that won her standing ovations. But no one who reads Hesser's book alongside the Stier Anderson Malone report (McGough 1996–2005) on the history of the IBT 743 can avoid wondering what Gina knew about what was going on around her. In the 1970s, when Gina went to work for 743, the president was mob-connected and under investigation. Hesser (2008) mentions Polk "dodging knives aimed at her back" and someone threatening to "throw her white bitch ass out a window" (56).

Then, after a huge mail-order house closed, she was assigned to state-sponsored job training programs for laid-off workers. Although this new assignment mostly took her away from relating directly with members, it attracted media attention. The beautiful, elegantly dressed young woman, who was a Teamster, made news. Only now was Gina invited to meet and talk with the executive board of the union where she had been working for nine years.

More than once, I have heard people who knew her say that if she had not been killed, Gina would have gone on to lead the union. Hesser (2008) quotes other people saying the same thing. This would have been a dangerous thing to say when she was alive — dangerous for Gina. It was not the kind of thing you would say about someone if you cared about what might happen to them. Hesser's book also mentions that during a period shortly before Polk's death, she had talked about decertifying the IBT at the University of Chicago and taking those workers into another union.

Hesser does not answer all the questions about Gina's death, but hers is as complete an account as we are going to get. Small plane crashes in bad weather in the Midwest are not unusual. In fact, many people avoid flying at that time for that reason.

After Gina's death, money was raised in her honour. Then the airline was sued, and Gina's widower, Tom Heagy, donated a large part of the settlement to a fund that became the Regina V. Polk Fund for Women's Labor Leadership. That was the money that I was allowed to spend on women's labour education conferences. And Gina's story was about leadership, its challenges and dangers, in a union where leadership was fiercely contested. With that as an origin story, what kind of women's conference was I going to run? What do we do with that legacy?

THE ORIGINAL CONFERENCE

The original idea for the Polk conference came from Helen Elkiss, who was my predecessor at the University of Illinois. During my hiring interview, she placed a brochure in front of me and underlined the name of the conference with a coloured marker: A Curriculum for Women Who Need to Refresh and Recover. "You have to do this!" she said. Helen, possibly thinking about how exhausted Regina must have been during those last years, started the Polk conference in 1988 as a retreat primarily for women leaders and staff, a place where they could relax and build trust with each other, to offset the overwhelmingly male culture of the Chicago labour movement in the 1990s. Helen limited the enrollment to twenty-five women. In 1999, my instinct was to go in a different direction.

A CURRICULUM FOR WOMEN WHO NEED TO FIGHT

Thanks to funding from the Polk Fund, I was able to work with Michelle Kaminski, a colleague at the University of Illinois until 2001, and a research assistant, Jocelyn Graf. We surveyed 250 women who had attended Polk between 1988 and 1999 (Worthen, Kaminski, and Graf 2005). We got ninety-nine responses, did forty-one phone interviews and came to some provocative findings. One finding was that, especially in low-wage occupations, women said that they did not have confidence in male leaders' ability to represent women members. This contrasted with women in higher-wage occupations, like office or professional work, who had more confidence in their male leaders. Another finding was that women said that, in order to become leaders themselves, they had to move up a ladder through many unpaid volunteer positions. For women, who typically had a "double shift" of work plus family responsibilities, a volunteer union position had to compete with cooking dinner and helping the kids with homework. Women could not justify spending their time that way. Therefore, as long as the ladder to leadership was through unpaid volunteer positions, this ladder did not exist for women. A third finding was how the demands of the double shift intersected in a woman's body. Paid or unpaid, both jobs were performed by the same body. So women's issues went way beyond being a sexual object. An injury to an elbow or a shoulder became a woman's issue when it prevented a woman from carrying out her gender-determined duties on the second shift. Carpal tunnel was a woman's issue when a woman could not make beds or wash dishes at home. Fatigue was a woman's issue if the mother was the person who supervised homework. Back or muscle injuries were a woman's issue if they prevented her from lifting a disabled parent or spouse.

REACHING OUT TO THE RANK AND FILE

Our findings helped us understand the women who came to Polk. It helped us see them, and ourselves, contextualized in a society that exploited women's commitment to their loved ones. The picture of women workers that this survey generated made me think about the unfulfilled leadership potential of rank and filers, and how much four days away from work and home might mean to such women. Therefore, I opened the conference to rank and file workers. I invited women to self-nominate. I wanted to include women who had not had time to climb the "volunteer" ladder. Focus on rank and file also meant that scholarships were not for staffers; staffers would be invited to come and teach, and sometimes get paid, but they would not take up scholarships needed by women who were coming on their own time. Nor did I require applicants to provide a reference from their union officers to show that they were being groomed for leadership. If there was a battle going on inside a union, I did outreach to the women to find those touched by the battle, on one side or another. I wanted as wide a range of industries, unions, ethnicities, colours, loyalties and first languages as possible, but I always made sure that there were women from the historically more democratic, activist unions and unions with a leftist leadership. The conference grew to forty-five and then to sixty-five women and more, if you include instructors.

A WHOLE-LIFE CURRICULUM FOR A WHOLE-LIFE STRUGGLE

The conference was a bubble, its own world. Four days — Thursday dinner through Sunday lunch — was enough so that women had the experience of being away from competing responsibilities, almost long enough to adapt to a different "normal." Criticisms of the conference were always "no down time" and "too intense," but it was that way intentionally. By opening the whole range of labour issues to a group that was entirely women, we made it possible for women to take any role, including ones like chief negotiators, ordinarily assumed by men.

So the question became, "What is the whole range of labour issues?" The answer: if you are working for wages in an economy that is not designed to protect you, everything you do is a labour issue. It is the necessary and inevitable condition of life in a capitalist economy. So, designing the conference around a smorgasbord of discrete classes in history, law, or skills would not wrap all of these together in a way that showed how they were all aspects of the same fight. The curriculum of labour education can be sorted into separate classes, and usually is, but I wanted Polk to roll the whole curriculum up into one continuous dramatic experience where, with plenty of instructors and coaches around, women could learn while acting out this struggle. It became half-theatre, half-game.

THE LONG-FORM ROLE-PLAYS

By 2002, I started to organize each conference around a long-form collective bargaining role-play. A role-play is kind of like acting out a case study, and Busman's (1981) work with using case studies in labour education provided guidance. "Long-form" is a term from stand-up comedy meaning extended improvisations. The forty-five-plus conference participants were divided into six teams of labour or management, with six or seven women on each side. The role-play would last two and a half days, with four bargaining sessions and a final presentation on the last day of the conference, during which the three teams would report and compare what they had been able to achieve. From the first dinner on Thursday night, when we distributed the background material for the role-play, all the way until Sunday morning, the clock was ticking. Each team chose a chief negotiator, a recorder and spokespeople for various issues. Each team had a coach. In addition to these "official" roles, women took roles in relationship to each other that had to do with how much they knew about what was going on: novice, learner, expert, critic, model, mentor, etc. The goal was to place women into different, close, transactional and ultimately transformational relationships with each other, in the hopes of helping them build a trust-bearing connection that would last after the conference was over.

At first, I wrote role-plays based on imaginary situations, but soon decided to use situations based on struggles that were currently going on, where the outcome was still unknown. I chose situations that were near enough geographically so that women actually involved in them could come. The first one of these long-form role-plays was based on a fight going on at a small non-profit mental health facility, Heartland Health Services, in Effingham, Illinois, where workers had gone on strike. With the help of women at Heartland I researched and wrote up the situation. Four of the Effingham women came to the conference, where, for the first bargaining session, they kept their identities a secret. When the secret burst out, it was a profoundly emotional experience for everyone. After that, the Effingham women at Polk became spokespersons for their fight throughout the Chicagoland labour movement and beyond, speaking at Labour Day and at the national convention of the American Federation of State, County and Municipal Employees.

A year later, in the midst of national debates about immigration, Polk brought in Leticia Zavala, vice-president of the Farm Labor Organizing Committee (FLOC). She arrived with her new baby and a young helper who happened to be undocumented, a word that was newly being used to replace "illegal." The role-play based on the FLOC situation was complicated by the fact that undocumented farm labourers are not covered by the National Labor Relations Act and FLOC in North Carolina first had to organize the growers into an employer association so that they would have someone to bargain with. The Polk women found themselves bargaining about the right to have guests in company housing, issues around seniority access to work visas and transportation for workers who go back to Mexico during the off-season. We had Spanish-speaking women from a workers' centre in Chicago at this conference, so we had simultaneous translation. This was also the year that Santiago Cruz, a young FLOC organizer who had been sent to Mexico to set up an office there, was murdered, probably by *coyotes* who wanted to profit by controlling the flow of workers across the border. Anne Feeney wrote a song about Cruz's murder.

Another year we had five women from the Republic Windows factory occupation with us. The role-play was a relatively simple one, but it allowed the Republic Windows women, who were UE members, to share their experiences as leaders in that occupation.

What Do People Learn from Extended Role-Plays?

One way to look at these collective bargaining role-plays is to compare them with the simulation exercises that are used in training firefighters, nurses, power-plant workers and others. These are workers whose lives depend on being able to suddenly deploy skills and implement practices in real life, simultaneously and in combination. They must combine all the separate skills and pieces of information into one single flowing action, carried out in a team. In training for these high-pressure jobs, workers practise in simulations. Although the struggle for decent jobs may not seem to require the kinds of teamwork practised by firefighters or emergency room nurses, in fact, it does. It requires people to act as a team, to be able to signal each other and read each other quickly, to move forward with commonly agreed upon actions, and to do so in a single flow — and in the face of serious opposition. Although skills like research, table behaviour and written communication can and should be studied as separate skills, rolling them all together into a single game or improvisation engages intelligence and emotion in a way that at least hints at what it will be like in real life.

WHAT ABOUT LEADERSHIP IN THE SENSE OF RUNNING FOR OFFICE?

In a conference about union leadership, one might expect that one of the topics would be how to run for office, but this is often not the case. Upcoming union leaders are usually groomed by incumbents, not taught in a class. One of the women in our 2000 survey shared, "If they don't want you, you can't run for dogcatcher." If someone is challenging an incumbent, they are left to figure out how to run on their own. For a college or university-based labour education program to offer such a class verges on interfering in internal union business.

However, to establish that this was really going to be a conference about women's leadership, we invited Linda Turney, who had just won the presidency of the Illinois Postal Workers Union, to come and tell us how she did it. She was happy to bring us the nitty-gritty of bumper stickers, pins, pens printed with her name and campaign slogan, and to teach us how to smile and shake hands up and down the state.

But a few years later, during a particularly tumultuous period in the internal politics of one union, I was accused of sympathy for the challenger and of "teaching union democracy" at Polk. The leadership threatened to organize a boycott of our labour education program, which would have had serious consequences. Our dean and the university attorney negotiated a compromise, which ultimately resulted in a visit to the conference itself by a male colleague, who evidently did not observe any union democracy and left early.

Nevertheless, if you are serious about teaching leadership, you cannot avoid teaching what the rungs on the ladders to leadership consist of and the very process of getting elected, which is a complex question addressed in union bylaws. Speaking as a citizen of the United States, I believe that for many people, their first conscious experience of democracy is through their union, if they are lucky enough to belong to one, not at the general election ballot box. Collective power becomes real right away in a union election. It may be the strike vote, the organizing vote, the contract ratification vote or the leadership election vote, but the connection between your vote and the money in your pocket is real. Then, win or lose, the experience of democracy can be transformative. Levels of fear go down. It is also durable. It feeds into other parts of a member's attitude. When a union is democratic, it shows in the way members behave. In their conversations, they "own" the issues that the union is fighting for. They speak for the leadership, saying "we" unselfconsciously, often without mentioning the names of their actual elected leaders. They act freely to take the initiative in describing what is going on in their unions and correct each other or fill in details in a way that indicates that there is no embargo on information and no hierarchy of who-gets-to-know-what.

Therefore, since we had to tread lightly on teaching union democracy explicitly, we always made sure to have participants from unions known to be democratic and give them an opportunity to talk about their experiences. Women from other unions, where things were much more controlled, would notice the difference and ask why.

ANNE FEENEY, HER MUSIC AND LABOUR ACTIVISM

Anne Feeney, whom Utah Phillips called "America's best labour singer," spent the last forty years travelling around the country showing up at rallies, strikes, picket lines and of course music festivals. This means that she has not only a great repertoire of songs (including "Have You Been to Jail for Justice?") but also a profound personal knowledge of what happened when and to whom. Except for one year when she was ill, she came to every Polk conference that I ran. She would arrive on the first day and stay until the very end, guitar in hand, participating in classes, organizing a labour chorus, sharing her knowledge of labour issues and history (she is also an attorney, an Industrial Workers of the World member and was president of the Pittsburgh musicians local for a brief time) and occasionally providing musical accompaniment to whatever drama was taking place.

One year we had a group of women from Machinists (IAM) Local 1487, which represents workers at United Airlines. Several of them had taken other classes with us. United Airlines had gone bankrupt and the bankruptcy court decided that it would permit the airline to default on pension benefits. Within the union, there was intense discussion about whether to go on strike or not. Theoretically, it would have been an illegal strike. A fight was brewing within the union.

As it happened, right after Polk, Anne Feeney had to go to Chicago's O'Hare airport and fly somewhere on United Airlines. She went to the gate for her flight, sat down, took out her guitar and began to sing rousing union songs, some especially tweaked for the audience of any IAM Local 1487 members who might be wandering through. One of the Polk women, Robyn Eulo, also left the conference and went to O'Hare, not to travel, but to do some union work. Anne was gathering a crowd and creating a disturbance when Robyn walked by and greeted her. The supervisor at the gate decided that the best way to handle the growing situation was to direct Robyn to bring it under control. The supervisor ordered Robyn "to make Anne Feeney stop singing." Robyn, who was not on the clock anyway, responded to the order by laughing out loud. "I can't make Anne Feeney stop singing!" she said (Eulo 2015).

This confrontation makes a good story, at least about Anne, but it had a long-term consequence for Robyn, who was disciplined for disobeying a direct order even though she was not on the clock. It took months for her grievance to wind its way through the grievance and arbitration procedure. Our goal at Polk to make current struggles connect with historic struggles often turned out to be only too easy.

THE TWO EDGES OF IMPACT: WHAT IF IMPACT IS A THREAT?

In order to justify the existence of women's conferences and women's programs, women labour educators are often asked to prove that women's labour education has an impact. The flip side of this is that we try to avoid making too much noise about impact because impact causes trouble. Note that I am writing this in retirement!

Polk has been a tempting object of study for the women who have taught at it or run it, perhaps because the participant list serves as a database of union women who are, for the most part, easy to reach. Helen Elkiss (1994) published an article about Polk in the *Labor Studies Journal*, in which she described the "glass ceiling" that women hit when they attempt to rise in their local union leadership. Emily Twarog, Jennifer Sherer, Brigid O'Farrell and Cheryl Coney (2016) and Emily Twarog (2016), current director of the Regina V. Polk Women's Labor Leadership Conference, also wrote about the impact of Polk. And now I'm writing this.

But how do you measure impact? A second survey by me and Michelle Kaminski produced another unpublished paper that demonstrated how women who had had labour education were less instrumentalist in their views of their unions (less "what have you done for me lately") than women who had not had labour education. Women who run the UALE summer schools always note that the self-reports written by women participants describe the experience as "transformative" or "empowering." However, the news that education has an impact and that a good education program has a strong impact is just common sense. Of course, education has an impact — why else do we do it?

The dark side, which only gets mentioned in passing, is that education that has a strong impact is a threat. Because of the close connection with Gina's union, IBT 743, famous for its leadership struggles, this may have been more apparent at the Polk conference than at other women's conferences. At Polk, with the story of Gina recounted tearfully year after year by people who knew her, the sense that new leadership means change is always hovering unsaid. Change can mean fresh brains and muscle stepping into the ranks to enable someone to retire. It can also mean a shake-up, complete with winners and unhappy, angry losers. For them, the less education the better, impact or not.

In 2002, quite a bit of money was awarded by the Polk Fund to the conference, perhaps more than we really needed. Emily Rosenberg and I proposed using it for a two-day gathering of all the women who had received Polk funding, in order to try and build a cohort with common values and ongoing coherence, identity and purpose. This would have given Polk women a collective voice and some visibility and leverage in the labour movement and the public realm beyond the conference. While this should not have been threatening to the Polk Fund, it was quickly rejected.

THE DRAMA OF WORK

There were many ways that I tried to make Polk a place where a woman's whole life could be engaged and respected. On a macro level, generous funding equalized what people had during those three days: food, classes, comfortable beds, a swimming pool and hot tub to relax in, and classes that created many different roles for each woman. The long-form role-play went on long enough to give everyone an important role as well as things to learn. Moving into a micro level, there was another activity that had the impact of binding a woman's body and her work together just as they are in real life, only now as spotlighted in a sixty-second performance, watched and applauded by her sisters at Polk.

This was not an ice-breaker, because you could not really do it on the first night of the conference. Instead, it was a good thing to do on the second night, when people already had a glimpse of each other as speakers, listeners, bodies sitting at tables, wearing their conference clothes. After dinner that second night, we would all go to a different room and form a circle. If there were sixty people at the conference, it would be a large circle. We would have chairs, because the activity was likely to last a long time. The idea was to perform — act out, dramatize — what you actually do at work, how you actually earn your living. Silently — no talking! People had been warned before the conference to bring their tools or equipment, and now, if they had remembered, they would have a chance to show what they did with them. Only gestures were allowed and there was a time limit of one minute, which was frequently exceeded. Each person would choose the next person to perform.

A mechanic showed how she changed a brake shoe. A food inspector found bugs in a basket of rolls. A fingerprint tech at the police department inked a suspect. A substitute teacher ducked and ran from a horde of wild eighth-graders. A plumber welded a pipe. A flight attendant showed us what she would do if we were on a plane about to crash. A sausage-maker stuffed sausages. Bus drivers broke up fights between passengers. English teachers sat, and sat, and sat, grading papers. A carpenter hung a door. A retired member demonstrated how she lay in a hammock and sipped a cold drink. The cashier you dealt with when you come to get your car that has been towed showed how she stayed calm and took your money, behind bulletproof glass. The labour educators also had to perform our work. It was like being in a dream of walking through the city and everyone in every workplace was a woman who knew what she was doing and did it well.

THE BODY AND THE JOB

When you see how people perform the physical actions that accomplish their work, you can see why their bodies become what they are. Because of their different jobs, women look even more diverse from each other when they are in action than when they are all sitting in a classroom. You can see how the movements of their work have shaped their bodies. You see a person reaching high and lifting something heavy, or moving fast, or trying to stay up late to get something written. Some of the women have long arms and big shoulders, or slumped shoulders, or hands as muscular and veiny as a man's or very soft and manicured. You can see why some of them are fat in certain places or thin in others. They have flat feet if they stand all day or bulging calves if they run back and forth. Some of them have special voices that they use at work, to say nothing of special smiles. They also have injuries, and some are in constant pain.

This exercise, performed by the circle of women each taking her turn in the centre, is a performance by everyone for an audience of everyone. It is a slap in the face for the idea that you can learn labour education by yourself with just your brain, or that you can be an outside expert and just watch. It underscores what we meant when we said, "Labour education is applied." It tells a truth about the struggle: it requires the whole heart and the whole body — and the rest of the women in the circle.

CHAPTER SEVEN

WILD IN MASSACHUSETTS

Leadership Development
for a Changing Labour Movement

Tess Ewing, Dale Melcher and Susan Winning

In 1985, a small group of women labour leaders and educators came up with the idea for creating a leadership program for union women in Massachusetts. The women had just attended the University and College Labor Education Association (UCLEA) Northeast Summer School for Union Women at the University of Massachusetts (UMass) Amherst, and while sitting under a tree processing the past week's work, they were inspired to replicate the summer school model for union women in Massachusetts, but in a shorter format and more accessible to a broader range of women. The Women's Institute for Leadership Development (WILD) emerged from this conversation.

We are three women deeply involved in and committed to the mission and work of WILD. One of us was a participant in the conversation under the tree in 1985, and one of us was WILD's director for eight years. We all are long-time active members of the WILD Board of Directors. We are either current or retired labour educators from the UMass labour extension program, which has partnered with WILD since its inception. Our commitment to WILD flows from its unique philosophy, inspiring vision, and work in the areas of leadership development, anti-racism/equity and popular education. In this examination of some of WILD's work we share best practices and challenges, present a model of an effective and sustainable leadership development program for labour movement women and reflect on thirty-one years of work in the field.

WHAT IS WILD?

WILD is a multiracial, multicultural, women's organization founded in 1986 to empower women, especially women of colour, to become effective activists, leaders and organizers in their workplaces and in the Massachusetts labour movement. For more than three decades WILD programs have provided educational and leadership opportunities, research and support to over 3,000 women in the Massachusetts economic justice movement.

WILD's founders brought to this work the support and resources of their organizations: the UMass labour programs at Amherst, Boston and Dartmouth, the Massachusetts American Federation of Labor-Congress of Industrial Organizations (AFL-CIO) and the Coalition of Labor Union Women (CLUW), which is a constituency group of the AFL-CIO. They engaged labour and women's movement leaders and activists in planning the first WILD summer institute in 1987. That first institute, held at Clark University in Worcester, Massachusetts, provided leadership and skills workshops, diversity sessions and cultural programming to about 125 women.

Building on the momentum from this successful first summer school, these women and their organizations established WILD as an ongoing program and articulated a mission that would guide its work. That original mission was four-fold:

- To increase the number and the diversity of women in leadership positions in the Massachusetts labour movement;
- To prioritize women's issues on unions' collective bargaining and political action agendas;
- To develop a model of women's leadership within the labour movement; and
- To create an educational model for women's leadership development that is relevant and accessible to working women and that is linked to an action strategy.

The first two points were a response to the demographics of organized labour in Massachusetts and to existing barriers to the participation of women. The Massachusetts labour movement had, and with a few notable exceptions still has, a predominantly white male leadership. Antagonism or indifference to issues of importance to women, as well as to other excluded or disenfranchised groups, was common. Significant barriers to women's advancement in leadership roles limited opportunities for women, and particularly women of colour. Language barriers further inhibited the participation of immigrant women. Even in unions where the majority of the members were women, leaders were by and large white men. The same was true in unions with significant numbers of members of colour. A 1991 study by the UMass Amherst Labor Center, commissioned by WILD, identified barriers to advancement that contributed to a wide disparity: women and people of colour were not represented in union leadership in proportion to their numbers in membership. Some of those barriers were societal in nature, having to do with cultural expectations of what is women's work, while some were more structural in nature, having to do with union organization and practices and entrenched male leadership. But WILD identified other barriers that it was well positioned to address, including knowledge and skills gaps, lack of role models and mentors, childcare responsibilities, inadequate union support for activism and leadership, and low self-confidence (Melcher, Eichstedt, Eriksen and Clawson 1992).

WILD has attempted to address these barriers, not only through the summer institute, but also through the WILD in the Winter program, which is a half-day conference, in both eastern and western Massachusetts. Additionally, WILD has developed leadership programs for individual unions, created mentoring opportunities, commissioned research and offered workshops and other programming in between the summer institutes.

WILD'S MISSION AND STRUCTURE

WILD's mission is a living document that is revisited each year as part of WILD's regular process of reflection and evaluation. WILD's current mission statement represents the evolution of our understanding of what it means to develop labour women's leadership in the context of an expansive definition of the labour movement. Two significant additions were made to the mission statement in 2000. The first defined the labour movement as including "not

---

WILD's Amended and Reaffirmed Mission

• Advocate for a vision of a labor movement that includes unions and all other organizations and people who join together to fight for the rights of working people and for social justice;

• Strengthen women's influence in the Massachusetts labor movement by increasing the number and diversity of women leaders, and providing them with tools to be effective organizers in their unions and organizations;

• Increase democratic participation in the labor movement, particularly among women and people of color;

• Help build a labor movement that operates from an activist rank-and-file perspective;

• Build awareness of and stimulate debate about issues of racism, sexism, class, homophobia and other issues of oppression within unions and the larger labor movement.

---

only unions, but also all other organizations and people who join together to fight for the rights of working people and for social justice." The second named homophobia as a source of oppression.

The evolving mission statement has also driven organizational change. In 1991, WILD incorporated as an independent non-profit, able to determine its own leadership board, hire staff and do its own fund-raising. The founders, themselves all white women, recognized that it would take a new structure, one not linked to the employees of the sponsoring organizations, to bring women of colour into the top level of leadership. Since 1991 WILD has had a diverse, activist board of directors, an annual budget currently over a hundred thousand dollars, a small staff and a variety of programs. However, even with staff and a modest budget, WILD has continued to rely on the contributions of some of the founding organizations and significant numbers of volunteers who participate in committees and assist with programs. While no longer organizational members, the female coordinators from the four UMass labour extension programs all play an active and critical role in the organization. The Boston CLUW chapter is no longer active, but the state labour federation has intermittently provided financial and outreach support.

As an organization with a board, staff and volunteers, and labour extension resources, WILD offers programs in addition to the summer institutes. This is a critical distinction from the United Association for Labor Education (UALE) women's summer schools, which rotate around each region and are planned and staffed by the host labour programs and union women who come together solely for the purpose of implementing each summer's school.

INTERCONNECTED THREADS

WILD's mission-guided work is best understood through examination of its leadership development and anti-oppression work and the use of popular education for both. All three aspects of WILD's work intersect and inform each other. For example, WILD's vision of the organizations and leaders we want to build puts an emphasis on internal democracy and development of a leadership body that fully represents the diversity of the membership. Anti-oppression education gives women ways to think about, and tools to tackle, the divisions created by racism and xenophobia, among other forms of marginalization and oppression. WILD's anti-oppression and leadership development programming has relied on the basic precepts of popular education, which create opportunities for conversations rooted in the collective sharing and analysis of lived experience and a focus on how to make change. WILD creates space to explore tensions and opportunities presented by the different experiences of working women as influenced by race, ethnicity, class, religion, sexual orientation and gender identification in order to build a stronger, more vibrant, labour movement.

In the following sections, we explore WILD's approach to leadership development and anti-oppression education and its use of popular education. We name the work, suggest why it is important and describe how WILD came to do it, a process that comes from continuity of organization and leadership coupled with an internal process of reflection, analysis and experimentation.

LEADERSHIP DEVELOPMENT

WILD's leadership development work is embedded in the organization's mission and the emergence of the WILDer vision. While the mission articulates why WILD exists, the WILDer vision describes the unions and organizations WILD women want to build and the kind of leadership we believe is needed to get us there. The WILDer vision developed from an activity in introductory leadership workshops in our early years, during which participants named the qualities and skills that make effective leaders and collaborated on drawings of what the leadership they aspire to looks like. These images — of quilts, trees, volcanoes, wheels and even loaves of bread — were shared as part of our Saturday evening program. Further discussions in relation to the lists and images, first in the curriculum committee and then on the board, resulted in the development of a statement that became the WILDer Vision of Unions and Community Organizations. The WILDer vision, which continues to evolve, is used in all leadership skills classes at the summer institute

---

Our WILDer Vision of Unions and Community Organizations

We work to build unions and organizations that are:

• Inclusive: recognizing the diversity of the membership and working to ensure that leadership reflects the make-up of the membership including language justice so that all are heard;

• Democratic: working to ensure that leadership and issues are chosen by the membership and are actively working to create opportunities for involvement by all members;

• Mobilizing: using internal organizing structures to communicate with and activate members;

• Fighting all forms of oppression: against women, people of color, lesbians, gays, bisexuals, transgender people and immigrants, and others who have been marginalized in the workplace, in our communities and in the union itself; and

• Organizing new members into the union, the community organization and the broader social and economic justice movement.

---

to stimulate discussion of effective leadership, the culture and practices of our own unions and organizations and how to make change.

Every summer institute offers two levels of leadership skills, reflecting the varied needs of both new and more experienced activists and leaders. The curricula are developed by a committee of volunteers who are, for the most part, labour educators from university, union and community-based programs, such as the Massachusetts Coalition for Occupational Safety and Health (MassCOSH) and United for a Fair Economy. Leadership B, for more experienced leaders, addresses a range of important leadership skills and is modified every year, while Leadership A is more consistent from year to year and addresses basic concepts of self-organization and action. Both levels of leadership include an action plan component, to help women take more leadership when they return to their unions or organizations. As our work evolved to embrace a broader definition of the labour movement, we revised our curriculum to incorporate the structure, work and issues of community-based social justice organizations. Developing leadership skills workshops which are meaningful to both union and community women has challenged us to recognize the differences and highlight the commonalities in work in two different but complementary arenas.

WILD offers a variety of skills and issues workshops to add to participants' leadership toolboxes. These include basic union skills, such as legal rights, bargaining and stewards training; individual skills, such as public speaking and conflict resolution; skills related to building effective community labour coalitions; and current issues, such as immigration and the economy. In between summer institutes, WILD offers workshops across the state that allow women to continue to network and develop their skills.

Learning without opportunities to practise has its limits. While we cannot guarantee that the unions and organizations that send women to WILD will encourage their activism and leadership, WILD itself can provide opportunities for exercising leadership. WILD women are recruited to participate in program planning and curriculum development, work on committees, speak at plenaries and help facilitate workshops. Recruiting new facilitators, training them in popular education theory and practice, and mentoring them for our leadership development workshops has, in fact, become an important opportunity for developing skills and increasing self-confidence. Volunteer work in all areas is a path to joining WILD's board and helping to guide the work of WILD. Volunteer power allows WILD to go beyond the limitations of a once-yearly weekend program and has become a key component of WILD's commitment to leadership development.

Part of the WILD vision is a definition of leadership that is collaborative. WILD's aim, beyond individual empowerment, is to confront the organizational structures and practices that obstruct women's leadership. In 1996, with funding support for three staff members, WILD developed Women Organizing Women, which the following year became WomenLead, a three-year leadership development and organizing project centred around organizing and building the effectiveness of women's committees at the state, regional and local union level. WILD partnered with the Massachusetts AFL-CIO Women's Committee and the UMass Labor Extension Program to provide training, support and networking opportunities to committees at several central labour councils (regional bodies of the AFL-CIO), the Northeast Regional Council of Carpenters and locals of several unions: the United Steelworkers (USW), the Service Employees International Union (SEIU), the International Union of Painters and Allied Trades and the International Brotherhood of Electrical Workers. After the formal program ended, some of the committees continued to function and have a close relationship with WILD.

WILD recognizes the key roles that mentors can play in leadership development and, to this end, has piloted several incarnations of a mentoring program. WILD Sisters, introduced at the 1997 summer institute, attempted to match volunteer mentors with women who wanted help taking on more leadership roles. However, without a support structure and an institutional relationship between mentors and mentees, WILD Sisters quickly faltered. Ten years later WILD launched Fit to Lead, which included a program for training mentors and another for bringing women together for several training sessions. While neither program was successful, the lessons that were learned through a reflective evaluation process informed the current mentoring program, which began in 2014. With support for additional staff through the Berger-Marks and Miller foundations, this program provides training and support for mentoring teams drawn from participating unions. Mentees set goals related to union work and then participate in WILD training sessions that support leadership development and the mentoring relationship. With some modifications, based on feedback from both mentors and mentees, the mentoring program has begun its second year with a new round of mentoring teams.

Popular Education

Central to its leadership development work is WILD's embrace of popular education as a way to educate and empower women, who will then see themselves as agents of collective action and change. While WILD's educational approach was always based on participation and engagement with learners' experiences, WILD came to popular education in 1994–95, when board members and teachers took workshops in the principles and practices of popular education. They recognized the value of an explicitly learner-centred, experience-based, participatory, problem-posing and social change-oriented approach. Popular education's roots in movements that strive to give voice to the voiceless and enfranchise marginalized peoples made popular education a perfect complement to WILD's vision and mission. The emphasis on education for change, for action, was particularly relevant to WILD's efforts to change the face of leadership in the Massachusetts labour movement, and the labour movement itself.

WILD formally embraced popular education as a guiding principle of curriculum development, program planning and teaching at the 1995 WILD board retreat. The board endorsed popular education training as a requirement first for all curriculum committee members and then for leadership facilitators, so that the leadership skills curricula (both A and B) would be based on popular education principles. Since then, basic and advanced popular education trainings have been offered not only to WILD teachers but also to other educators in the social and economic justice movement. In 2015, twenty-six women from eighteen groups, including unions and community-based organizations, attended a basic and advanced, day-long, popular education training session, which included exposure to WILD's most recent leadership skills curriculum. Several participants taught for the first time at the 2015 summer institute.

ANTI-RACISM AND ANTI-OPPRESSION WORK

Education that challenges racism has been one of WILD's core commitments since the beginning. The founding members of WILD were staunch anti-racists. They knew that the kind of change they wanted to see in the labour movement would not be accomplished by elevating a few white women into leadership positions under the same old rules. Rather, they knew it would require a complete cultural shift, one that would include all the groups that had traditionally been excluded from power working together. Given the persistent pervasiveness of racism in our society and the overwhelming whiteness of the traditional Massachusetts labour movement, the WILD board knows that efforts to combat racism will require constant, ongoing attention, a willingness to explore various approaches and the courage to push back against resistance.

The WILD Board and Staff

Anti-oppression work has taken place in both the content of WILD programs and in the internal structure of the organization. WILD has committed to having a board in which at least half of the members are women of colour. The current board of sixteen is made up of eight women of colour, including African-American, African, Haitian, Latina and Afro-Brazilian women, and eight white women. The current board president is African-American. Recently, WILD reconstituted an advisory board, made up of a diverse group of influential women in the Massachusetts labour movement. The advisory board provides advice and support without overpowering the voice of the rank and file activists on the board. Women of colour on the advisory board are also role models for all WILD women.

Formal racial balance on the board is, however, only a first step. There is recognition that white board members have, in general, more informal influence and power at the board level because they have tended to bring with them all the privileges of a more middle-class upbringing, including more education and more experience in the labour movement. The UMass labour educators, for example, are all white women who have had the support of their programs, allowing them to bring their expertise as well as time and resources to their WILD work. Consequently, for them, WILD work is a part of their workload. No women of colour on the board have such resources at their disposal. WILD has challenged this power imbalance in many ways, including sending multiracial teams of board members to anti-racism trainings, working with diversity consultants and making sure the anti-oppression messages developed and taught in WILD's programs are also applied within the organization. Conflicts on the board are often described in non-racial terms, such as being between seasoned and new board members, or being personality clashes. However, the board is cognizant of the fact that often, as one woman put it, "even when it's not about race, it's about race." It is an ongoing effort and one that the WILD board is aware will never be completely over while racism exists within the larger society.

Besides the attention to the composition of the board, WILD has tried, with limited success, to hire staff of colour. At one point in the late 1990s and early 2000s, WILD had enough money for a staff of three, which included two organizers, who were a Latina and an African-American woman, and a director, who was a white woman. During the recession, grant money and donor support shrank, and the staff was reduced to a permanent full-time or part-time director and a temporary part-time assistant, who helps organize and run the summer institute. With the exception of one short period when WILD had an African-American director, the director has been a white woman. The part-time assistant has been a Latina. With funding from the Miller Foundation, WILD has recently been able to significantly raise the number of hours that it can pay this part-time staff person. This year she was hired in the fall and is able to assist in the mentoring program and do more outreach with Latinas.

THE SUMMER INSTITUTE

Perhaps the best way to get an idea of how WILD incorporates its anti-racist agenda into its programs is to see how it works during a typical summer institute. On the afternoon of June 20, 2014, some 110 women from across the state converged on the campus of UMass Dartmouth, in southeastern

Massachusetts. About 65 percent were women of colour, including significant numbers of Spanish- and Portuguese-speaking women. They ranged in age from early twenties to late seventies. Some brought children, supported by our childcare program. They came from over a dozen union locals and another dozen community organizations.

Friday Evening

After signing in, getting settled in their rooms, eating supper and taking their children to childcare, the women congregated in the main meeting room for the Friday night program. Everyone was given a headset. This session, like the other plenary sessions throughout the weekend, was conducted in English, Spanish and Portuguese, with simultaneous interpretation for all. The emcees were a Haitian-American woman and a Latina. The Friday night program included an icebreaker, a welcome speech from a local woman labour leader, some background about the history and philosophy of WILD and a bit about what to expect for the weekend.

An important piece here was the explanation of the caucus meetings that would take place on Saturday. At every summer institute WILD provided time and space for women to share an identity that is less powerful, or less recognized, or discriminated against to meet, and if they choose, to report back to the body on Saturday evening about their issues as a group. Participation is optional. The number and identities of the caucuses has varied somewhat over the years, but the current practice is to set up five — three based on racial/ethnic identity and two focused on other aspects of identity. Women are given the opportunity on Friday night to organize other caucuses if they want. If three women sign up for a new caucus, a room will be provided. The caucuses meet at two different times, so women can choose up to two caucuses to attend. After the presentations, there was a participatory exercise on the growth and impact of economic inequality, followed by some rousing songs.

Saturday Workshops and Caucuses

On Saturday morning, the participants all started with a leadership workshop, either Leadership A or Leadership B. At both levels, there was a leadership workshop taught in Spanish, and one taught bilingually in Portuguese and English, as well as one or more solely in English. All workshops were co-taught by two teachers, with the goals of pairing an experienced teacher with a newer one, and to have the pairs be racially mixed. These goals were met for most of the leadership workshops.

After the leadership class, everyone came back together for a two-hour anti-oppression session, which varies from year to year. It usually focuses on racism, but includes other forms of oppression as well, and it seeks to uncover the institutional nature of oppression, as opposed to personal prejudices. In 2014, the anti-oppression workshop took the form of a participatory exercise,

---

Celebrating Our Differences, Building Our Unity

In order to provide responsive, energetic and visionary leadership in the decades to come, unions must mobilize women workers and encourage and develop women as leaders.

We believe that as a necessary first step towards reaching this goal, it is important for WILD to provide the opportunity for women from all backgrounds and experiences to acknowledge and explore our unique identities and various cultural heritages.

Our clear vision and enthusiasm to lead are rooted in taking pride in who we are and valuing our differences.

At the same time, we increase our strength by celebrating our unity and solidarity as women workers.

---

based on shared stories, aimed at making the personal impact of institutional and cultural racism visible on a personal level and allowing for the sometimes emotional processing of the stories.

This activity was part of WILD's ongoing commitment to have a session devoted to building a multiracial, multicultural labour movement. WILD's understanding of the issue, as well as the format of the session, has changed over the years. At first, concerned with alienating some summer institute participants, WILD couched this part of the program in the language of diversity and inclusion. The early diversity statement, given to all participants, made no mention of power inequality. (See Box: Celebrating Our Differences, Building Our Unity.) From 1994 to 1999, WILD offered an optional skills workshop called Fighting Racism in the Workplace and Union. Then for a few years, the anti-racism segment was incorporated into the leadership workshops. For the last several years, WILD has returned to the stand-alone plenary format, with all women participating in the same activity together. This segment changes each year as WILD seeks effective, relevant and timely ways to engage in this conversation.

The next activity, after lunch, was the first round of caucus meetings. Caucuses for Women of African Heritage, Latinas and Brazilians met at this time. The other two, one for lesbian, gay, bisexual, transgender and queer (LGBTQ) women and one for young women, met after the afternoon workshops. Caucuses are offered the opportunity to present during the Saturday evening program. The caucus reports are limited to two minutes per caucus and are encouraged to answer the following two questions: What issues does your group face in the labour movement and in your community? What would your caucus group like your WILD sisters to know about and/or do to support your group and your group's issues?

The afternoon workshops, which meet on both Saturday and Sunday, are on specific skills or issues, and participants choose which one to attend. In 2014, there were four English-only workshops, one bilingual English/Spanish workshop, and two bilingual Spanish/Portuguese workshops. The Saturday evening program began with caucus reports. Some were quite moving and opened WILD participants' eyes and hearts to the obstacles some of our sisters face. The cultural program that followed featured a local young woman of colour who is a spoken word artist. When the formal program ended, the DJ set up her equipment, the lights were dimmed and the dance party began. The party is always a WILD highlight. The DJ, who has been providing the music for many years, has built up a collection of U.S., Latin American and Brazilian music that keeps everyone out on the dance floor.

Sunday Workshops and Graduation

On Sunday, the leadership and skills workshops each had their second two-hour session, followed by a graduation lunch. The graduation speaker was a dynamic Latina leader of an SEIU organizing drive. In inviting outside speakers and entertainers, as well as emcees and facilitators from among its own ranks, WILD tries to model its commitment to inclusion by choosing women from diverse racial, ethnic and cultural backgrounds. The graduation lunch, like the Friday and Saturday evening programs, is conducted and simultaneously interpreted in three languages.

LANGUAGE JUSTICE

WILD's commitment to making the summer institute accessible to Spanish- and Portuguese-speaking women merits a closer examination. The first Spanish-language workshop was offered in the early 1990s. Some WILD activists were working with unions that represented significant numbers of Latinx and with the Immigrant Workers Resource Center, a local union-sponsored immigrant workers' centre. Initially, bilingual participant volunteers translated for the Latina sisters, but within a few years, these volunteers pushed WILD to hire professional interpreters, as it was impossible to both participate and translate. The WILD board discussed adding other languages in the next few years but decided not to. Providing workshops in other languages, translating materials and providing interpretation for plenary sessions takes a considerable outlay of both time and money — resources WILD did not have.

The next step forward came in the late 1990s and early 2000s when the hitherto tiny Brazilian population of eastern Massachusetts grew into one of the area's largest immigrant groups. And they were organized. In 2005, a bilingual Brazilian participant offered to bring Portuguese-speaking women to WILD and volunteered to interpret for them. As with Spanish, after the first years using volunteers, WILD now hires professional interpreters for Portuguese.

Each year WILD offers several workshop choices for Spanish- and Portuguese-speaking participants. Still, it has been a challenge to fully integrate Spanish- and Portuguese-speaking participants into the summer institute. Outside of the workshops and the caucuses, they tended to spend time with only other speakers of their language. During the plenary sessions, they sat in groups with their headsets on while the English speakers were able to participate more fully. This led to WILD's commitment, as of 2012, to strive for language justice — to make WILD a fully trilingual weekend. In addition to offering bi- and trilingual workshops, WILD moved to simultaneous interpretation in three languages, where everyone wears headsets and speakers are invited to speak in the language they are most comfortable with. Although language justice is an aspirational goal, WILD cannot fully accommodate all of the many languages spoken in Massachusetts. Even among the three languages that are spoken at the summer institute, English will predominate. Still, WILD feels that the effort has significantly expanded the participation of immigrant women.

THE INTERSECTION OF IMMIGRATION AND RACISM

A further step in addressing the needs of immigrant women and exploring the connections between immigrant issues and racism happened at the 2013 summer institute. One hundred and fifty women sat in a large room to talk about immigrant rights and the intersection of racism and immigration policy. Black, white and Latina women, whose first languages were English, Spanish and Portuguese, were encouraged to sit at tables with women they did not know, with some tables designated as monolingual and some as bilingual, to facilitate discussion.

The conversation began with stories. Facilitators introduced the conversation by sharing their family stories of immigration, establishing that, with the exception of Indigenous Peoples, we are all immigrants. The next story was a TED (Technology, Entertainment, Design) talk video by U.S. journalist Jose Antonio Vargas on his experience of being an undocumented immigrant. Following the video, member-leaders of Just Communities, an immigrant organizing project, shared their stories. At their tables, women then used a set of questions that invited them to synthesize and analyze the Vargas talk, to respond to one of the key questions on the immigration debate that he poses and to bring their life experiences to bear on their conversation. Finally, they considered the connections between anti-immigrant sentiment and actions and homegrown American racism.

This was the first time WILD used the anti-oppression plenary to focus on immigration. July 2013 was a critical moment in relation to U.S. immigration reform. The U.S. Senate had just passed an immigration reform bill and debate had started in the U.S. House of Representatives. While there was no expectation the bill would become law, it was clearly a moment for national conversation and for activism.

The conversation on immigration and racism was deeply moving. The stories personalized the immigration experience in the United States. The Vargas video powerfully laid out the reality for undocumented Americans and made connections to America's historical racism. The Just Communities women's stories were equally powerful in their immediacy. During the report-back more women stood to share their personal and family immigration experiences. The session closed with a call to action on two pieces of proposed Massachusetts's legislation that would directly address important issues for immigrants — the notification of U.S. Immigration and Customs Enforcement by local police after routine traffic stops and the inability to get a driver's licence without proof of legal residency.

The immigration conversation also reflected the power of using a popular education approach — telling stories and sharing experiences, synthesizing and analyzing those experiences, collectively creating new knowledge, and then planning for action. The activity emphasized the value of the experience in the room and the importance of going beyond what we collectively know by adding new information, in this case, the Vargas talk and the presentation on the proposed immigration reform legislation. Simultaneous interpretation made the experience a truly shared one and made visible to English speakers both the challenge and the importance of language justice. Finally, participants pledged to take leadership on this issue and move members to take action in support of the legislation.

BEYOND THE SUMMER INSTITUTE

While the summer institute is WILD's signature program, it is not the only vehicle for challenging various forms of oppression. For several years, the women who attended the Latina caucus and the Women of African Heritage (WOAH) caucus at the summer institute continued to meet periodically throughout the year. In 2001 the WOAH caucus developed a project called the Women of African Heritage Leadership Project, which involved ongoing training during the months between summer institutes. Another important though short-lived effort, the Black and Brown Project, was the brainchild of an African-American and a Latina board member. Its purpose was to bring African-American women and Latinas together to learn about each other's histories and struggles and to work through some of the tensions between the two groups.

WILD has several times partnered with other organizations to help advance the rights of immigrant women. WILD was one of the five founding organizations, in 2010, of the Massachusetts Coalition for Domestic Workers, which recently fought for and won passage of legislation protecting the rights of domestic workers in the state. Past partnerships include two projects to provide training on workers' rights and leadership development to immigrant women, one with the Immigrant Workers Resource Center (1997–2001) and one with SEIU Local 615, the building services local, in 2002.

WILD efforts to recruit immigrant women outside of unions were initially driven by the desire to bring in more Latina participants. In Massachusetts in the 1990s, many organized Latinx were in an SEIU building services union that was roundly mistrusted and disliked by its Latinx members for its racist and corrupt leadership. This same local's leadership refused to send any of its members to WILD. The local was large enough, and had enough Latinx members, that it poisoned the atmosphere in the Boston area Latinx community about unions in general. At the time, WILD had a Latina organizer who found that the best way to reach Latinas, even union members, was through community-based organizations, and particularly immigrant organizations. This work with low-wage Latina workers, both union and non-union, plus pressure from a WILD Latina organizer, who was a native of El Salvador — where the definition of the labour movement includes non-union workers — led to embracing a definition of the labour movement that included worker centres and other community-based organizations.

WILD now recruits women for all its programs from a broad range of organizations. These include community groups that organize and promote workers' rights (often referred to as alternative labour or alt-labour), such as the Brazilian Worker Center, MassCOSH Worker Center, the Dominican Development Center and Vida Verde (a Brazilian housecleaners' cooperative), as well as other social and economic justice organizations, such as Jobs with Justice, immigrant organizing groups and anti-foreclosure activists. These women are overwhelmingly women of colour, many of them recent immigrants. They bring unique perspectives to conversations about leadership and anti-oppression work. Our challenge is to provide curriculum and programming that is meaningful to both union and community women and to facilitate conversation between the two groups. There is tremendous potential for developing women leaders in community organizations, but for WILD this work must be done alongside efforts to develop more activists and leaders in the ranks of organized labour.

WILD'S SUCCESSES

WILD has much to be proud of. The fact that it has managed to survive for more than thirty years as an independent organization without institutional sponsorship, at a time when organized labour's numbers and resources have been steadily declining, is an accomplishment in itself. We have held a summer institute every single year since 1987. We have held WILD in the Winter programs and popular education teacher training workshops almost every year since the mid-1990s. We have conducted stand-alone workshops; we have organized mentoring programs; we have partnered with unions and immigrant organizations to train their leaders; and we have participated in coalitions. During the three decades of WILD's existence, some 3,000 women have come through our programs. These have ranged from rank and file union members who had never thought of becoming leaders, to some of the top female union leaders in Massachusetts.

Over the years, WILD has become respected and recognized as a valuable resource by unions, central labour councils and the state federation, alt-labour groups and other social and economic justice organizations. We have raised the profile of leadership by women and people of colour within the house of labour in Massachusetts. We have championed and attempted to embody a particular vision of leadership and of the type of organizations that we want to build: inclusive, representative, democratic and activist. By bringing together women from different unions and organizations, including across language barriers, WILD has helped forge links between traditional organized labour and alt-labour, and among worker centres, immigrant groups and other economic and social justice organizations. WILD is one of the few places where women can meet and share ideas and practices with others who are working for similar goals in different contexts.

Measured against the goals of its founders, WILD has succeeded well in those areas over which it has had control. As noted earlier, the original mission had four points. Taking the last two points first, WILD has indeed developed a model for women's leadership, which is summed up in the WILDer Vision of Unions and Community Organizations. It has developed an educational model through the mix of the summer institutes and other educational events, opportunities for putting the learning into practice in WILD committees and other activities, mentoring programs and the practice of popular education. The weekend format of the summer institute, the childcare, the scholarships and the translation/interpretation have made the institute accessible to a wide range of working women with limited means. And WILD's educational programs are always linked to action. An advantage of our relatively narrow geographical scope is that women can be drawn into local and regional organizing or political campaigns.

The extent to which WILD has succeeded in accomplishing the goals that are less under its control is harder to measure. Certainly, there are more women in leadership positions in the Massachusetts labour movement than there were in 1987. We like to believe that, in addition to larger societal changes, WILD's influence is partly responsible for this increase. The top leadership of the Massachusetts labour movement continues to be largely white. We know of WILD women of colour who have become stewards or executive board members of their locals, taken on leadership roles in their organizations and even run for municipal or state office. An African-American WILD alumna and former board member is now president of a large SEIU local. The number of women on the Massachusetts AFL-CIO Executive Council has increased, including many who identify as WILD women and/or publicly support WILD. Women in their program evaluations cite their experience at WILD as critical to their development and advancement as union leaders (Enwright, McGlinn and Juravich 1996). WILD graduates have played a part in prioritizing women's issues in collective bargaining and union political agendas. Massachusetts unions are now deeply involved in legislative campaigns that are important to women — paid sick days, domestic workers' rights, paid parental leave and protections for pregnant workers. While some of this reflects changes in the labour movement of the past years, we believe WILD's contribution has been significant.

Many factors contribute to someone becoming a leader or to a union deciding to take up a given issue; it is impossible to tease out what can be traced to participation in WILD (Catlett 1986). WILD clearly has helped women take their own next steps, gain self-confidence, learn new skills, make connections and share experiences, strategies and practices. WILD has played a role in the growing openness of the Massachusetts labour movement to women as leaders and to women's issues.

CONTINUING CHALLENGES

WILD, like other social justice groups, faces significant challenges. Perhaps the most critical is how to ensure sustainability of both people and funding. The generation of women who founded WILD has played a vital role in the organization. Many of those women are now retired. Although they continue to be active, the time will come when they will pull back from volunteer work. Of crucial importance has been the part played by the UMass Labor Extension Program, which has had a *de facto* partnership with WILD since the program began in 1995. New extension staff may not be women or desire to be as deeply involved in WILD as our colleagues and we have been. The crossroads that many small organizations face when transitioning from their founders to a new generation of leaders is compounded by a very possible loss of tangible resources.

Funding is our second sustainability challenge. Like so many other small non-profits, WILD has to work hard every year to raise its budget. Our funding comes from three sources: foundation grants, donations — from individuals, unions and other organizations — and income from programs. As traditional union membership declines WILD participation by women from alt-labour organizations has increased. These organizations do not have the resources to send members, increasing the demand for scholarships. WILD has tried, unsuccessfully, to develop its own dues-paying membership base, but has defaulted to our original pattern: those who can, donate; those who can't, don't.

We depend on the limited number of foundations that fund labour-related causes and a few generous donors. When one of these foundations, which tend to be small themselves, changes its funding priorities or skips a funding cycle, we suffer. And our major donors are aging as well. Working with a shoestring budget makes it hard to fulfill our mission, particularly as it relates to promoting the leadership of low income women and women of colour. Simultaneous interpretation and childcare are expensive. Scholarships seriously eat into our summer institute revenue. Finally, our limited resources make it difficult to build sustainable staff diversity

There are other challenges that stem from our expanded definition of the labour movement, particularly in the areas of programming and curriculum. How do we design workshops that are relevant to both women covered by collective bargaining agreements and those who are not? Union women still need to learn how to negotiate a contract or be an effective steward, as well as skills that are more easily transferable to non-union settings.

The labour movement is changing and WILD is proud to be not only part of that change, but also usually well ahead of the curve. The evolution of our mission statement over the years has reflected our understanding of and adaptation to that change. The workforce has become much more diverse, and WILD has emphasized building diverse leadership and fighting discrimination. Immigrants comprise a larger share of the workforce, and WILD has pioneered striving for language justice in the labour movement. The right-wing onslaught against unions has crippled the traditional legal mechanisms for addressing workers' concerns, and WILD has emphasized activist, rank and file, democratic unionism. Unions themselves have lost ground while new alternative forms of worker organization have sprung up, and WILD has expanded its definition of the labour movement. We cannot predict what tomorrow will bring for WILD or for the labour movement. WILD has shown remarkable flexibility through its practice of ongoing evaluation of all its programs and revision of those programs, where necessary. This practice will stand it in good stead as the organization faces a continually changing future.

CHAPTER EIGHT

LEADERS FOR TOMORROW
Promoting Diverse Leadership in ETFO

Carol Zavitz

Leaders for Tomorrow (L4T) is an initiative of the Elementary Teachers' Federation of Ontario (ETFO). Since its inception in 2004, this program has invited women ETFO members from "designated groups" (Indigenous, disabled, LGBTQ and/or racialized) to partake in a full-year, multisession course designed to equip them with the skills, knowledge and networks needed to access leadership positions within the union. L4T is rooted in feminist and progressive activism within ETFO and its predecessors. Three hundred and ten women have participated in this program in fifteen years, and for many of them, the experience has been transformative. I was involved in developing and running L4T for its first six years, and I acknowledge the other staff and members whose collective efforts made the program possible.

ETFO'S FEMINIST ROOTS

ETFO is the largest teachers' union in Canada, representing 81,000 teachers and education professionals working in Ontario public elementary schools.[1] ETFO is a relatively new union with a long history. It was born in 1998 when the Federation of Women Teachers' Associations of Ontario (FWTAO) and the Ontario Public School Teachers' Federation (OPSTF) merged. Organized in the era of women's suffrage, FWTAO was, from the outset, committed to women's equality in education and society and represented women elementary teachers, vice-principals and principals. OPSTF was founded in 1920 and represented male elementary teachers and administrators. From very early in its existence, OPSTF's vision of its future included an amalgamation with FWTAO. FWTAO was not interested in amalgamation, believing that women's perspectives and voices would be lost in any merged organization. Unable to convince FWTAO to amalgamate, OPSTF initiated several different legal strategies over the years that ultimately, combined with changing political circumstances in Ontario, led to formal merger discussions in 1996.

The two unions negotiated a new constitution that carried on the feminist perspective of FWTAO. One of three vice-presidents and four of the ten members of the provincial executive must be women. In addition, 6 percent of the union's overall annual budget is allocated to programs for women, including donations for both Canadian and international women's organizations. Time will tell if the merger improved the lot of women elementary teachers in Ontario. The first president and general secretary of ETFO were both from OPSTF, which seemed to confirm the fears of FWTAO activists that women's voices would be lost in the new union. The end of FWTAO was seen in some quarters as a blow to the Canadian women's movement (Spagnuolo and Glassford 2008). Michelle Landsberg (2011: 273–274) expressed this view as follows:

> The FW[TAO] was a lively source of money and support for feminist causes. It helped raise money for LEAF, the legal fund that took important cases to the Supreme Court; it backed the lobbying efforts around the Constitution; it funded hundreds of feminist meetings, conferences, films, books and research reports; it produced sparkling materials for schools about women's rights and women's history; it supported gun control, gave women teachers scholarships to teach leadership skills abroad, fought for better pensions for women, and promoted the careers and interests of tens of thousands of women teachers, helping crash through barriers erected by the men in power.
>
> The FW[TAO] was a pioneer in fighting for equity and social justice issues; it was out front in its ten-year struggle for better child care; another decade of effort went into naming and battling violence against women. FW, as it was affectionately known, gave all of us confidence and courage—it was so big, so intelligent, and so strong.
>
> When people talk about why the National Action Committee on the Status of Women finally lapsed into insignificance, or why the women's movement began to lose steam, the crushing of FW is one of the reasons that remains largely unremarked.

BUILDING FOR TOMORROW

In 2003, ETFO began an ambitious expansion of its capacity for collective bargaining. This program, branded "Building for Tomorrow," resulted in staffing increases in collective bargaining and the creation of an extensive training program for local presidents and chief negotiators. The brand new union went through several years of brutal bargaining; thirty-one of the thirty-nine elementary strikes (including work to rule, rotating strikes, etc.) since 1975 took place after the election of the Mike Harris government in Ontario in 1995. With a new government, and determined to bargain back what had been lost during the Harris years, the ETFO decision to concentrate on growing its collective bargaining capacity had broad membership support. However, focusing training and other resources on members involved in collective bargaining and holding local elected office meant focusing on a disproportionately male group of members.

ETFO created its Equity and Women's Services (EWS) department in 1999, to support its constitutional objective "to foster a climate of social justice in Ontario and continue a leadership role in such areas as anti-poverty, non-violence, and equity."[2] Staff in EWS began reporting on the participation of women and members from "designated groups" (Indigenous, disabled, LGBTQ and racialized) in ETFO activities and leadership positions, and kept track of the numbers of women and men speaking at decision-making meetings. By 2003, it was clear that women were seriously under-represented in local leadership and collective bargaining roles. Eighty-one percent of ETFO members were women, but in 2004 only 64 percent of local presidents and 44 percent of local chief negotiators were women.[3] Members from designated groups were much less present in leadership positions. The Leadership for Tomorrow program was introduced in 2004 to address these issues. The year-long program was designed for women members who self-identified as Indigenous, disabled, LGBTQ and/or racialized.

FOUNDATIONS OF LEADERSHIP FOR TOMORROW, 2004–2010

In its first five years (1998–2003), ETFO developed strong foundational policies addressing a broad range of equity issues. Several leadership programs for women members and members from equity-seeking groups, mostly short workshops and conferences, were already available in 2004. Consolidating budgets from some of these existing programs for women, staff in EWS designed Leadership for Tomorrow, in consultation with a professional coach. The objectives of L4T were the following:

- to provide information, strategies, supports and skills to women from designated groups to enhance their leadership abilities;
- to encourage participants to expand their leadership roles with ETFO in the provincial and/or local political arena;
- to encourage participants to prepare and apply for senior staff positions within ETFO; and
- to foster a community of diverse women within the federation to ensure their voices are heard and their issues are addressed.

All four executive staff from EWS were involved in designing and presenting the course for its first two years: two straight White women (permanent staff of long tenure), a straight racialized woman (permanent staff) and a straight Indigenous woman (temporary staff), all able-bodied, shared decision-making and attended all sessions. Our diversity, including different personalities, leadership styles and backgrounds, offered a range of models for participants.

In those first two years (2004–06), many of the lasting features of L4T were established. The course addressed issues of identity, oppression and intersectionality; the history of the women's movement; First Nations, Métis and Inuit (FNMI) issues; personal and interpersonal leadership values and styles; ETFO structures and processes; and physical and spiritual wellness. We organized sessions with women leaders in ETFO and other organizations, exploring their individual paths to leadership and their personal struggles with systemic and institutional discrimination. We role-played collective bargaining situations, election speeches, local executive meetings and holding courageous conversations. Through daily written feedback and "circle time," participants discussed the broader context of our union and the workplace, as well as addressing barriers and biases arising within the group. During a culminating activity, participants shared "identity pieces" produced in the media of their choice. And L4T participants continued their learning in the outside world, attending ETFO's annual conference for women members, where they helped host or present in workshops, and observed ETFO's representative council and/or provincial executive. L4T graduates also acted as mentors to participants for the following year. For several years, an annual reunion was held, to ensure that participants stayed in touch with ETFO and with each other.

Members' expenses, including travel and accommodation, time off work and dependent-care expenses, are paid by the union. Originally, we scheduled evening and weekend sessions and long days, to get members used to the time demands of union leadership and to facilitate the development of coping mechanisms and practical solutions to being away from home. We intentionally created conditions similar to those found in union leadership roles: long hours, unexpected assignments and unreasonable deadlines. Participants were asked to thank speakers at the last moment, so they would be used to thinking on their feet. We assigned roles to challenge members in the collective bargaining and executive role-plays. Participants were expected to attend dinners and social time and get to know each other outside the formal setting. We assigned homework for most sessions and expected everyone to give year-end presentations.

Working with Diverse Groups

What has always been unique about L4T is the deliberate diversity of the group; only women who self-identified as members of equity-seeking groups were admitted to the program. Some of them were contacted about the course because they had already self-identified while others saw the flier and applied, self-identifying in that process. These women came into the room curious about each other but hesitant to ask direct questions about each other's identities. Kristin Schwartz (2009: 23) described it this way:

> People are very raw. Their frustration and anxiety about discrimina-
> tion or barriers they've had to deal with — it comes right out. Some
> people are yelling, some are crying, there is shakiness in their voices.
> The Black women sit with each other, the Aboriginal women sit
> together, the women who identify as LGBT. The filters aren't there
> and the facilitators encourage you to be very honest.

In the first year, we held the workshop on identity, oppression and collective responsibility during the final session, which turned out to be a mistake. In subsequent years, we scheduled it in the first session and opened up deep and wide conversations about identity that lasted all year. The group composition was different every year. One year, almost all the racialized women were Christians and almost all the White women were lesbians. The dynamics that year were frequently very tense as the women worked through negative attitudes they had brought into the group and shared experiences and perspectives. Women ended the program with some surprising friendships and a strong sense of group solidarity.

One consistent feature was the very small number of Indigenous participants.[4] Despite staff outreach efforts, most years there would be only one or two Indigenous women in the course, who often expressed feelings of isolation. Every year, the program included an Indigenous component in most sessions, sometimes facilitated by staff or current member(s) of the course, sometimes by graduates from previous years, sometimes by outside facilitators. I especially remember a sunrise ceremony on the shore of Lake Ontario at the end of the second year. A 2006 participant gave this feedback:

> It was so very fitting to culminate our time together with the placing
> of the tobacco in the sacred fire, as a single, beautiful, white swan
> silently flew by. She was a tangible, albeit surreal representation
> of each of us leaving the "nest" of L4T to take flight as leaders in
> each of our lives.

The Power of Role-Playing

Everyone has their own style of learning, and so L4T varied its instructional strategies, including lectures, discussions, arts and role-playing. Participants usually groan when it is time to engage in role-plays, but learn surprising and important things about themselves. Many memorable L4T moments occurred during these exercises, but a couple of events during the collective bargaining role-plays stand out.

Staff developed a practice of assigning the role of chief negotiator to a participant who seemed to be holding back, as a challenge to that woman. In one case, when a particular chief negotiator first faced the employer, she experienced real difficulty. The women assuming the roles of the employers were asked to perform a hit parade of all the clueless, bullying, unprepared and obnoxious employer negotiators they had ever seen, and as experienced union negotiators they had seen a lot. The member playing the chief negotiator was shocked; she was interrupted, disrespected, condescended to and bullied. Her own caucus was getting increasingly nervous and was showering her with helpful notes about what to say. She was obviously flustered, and it looked as though the session would be a rout for the union side, when she suddenly drew herself up straight. With a voice much louder and clearer than her usual voice, she called out the other side's rudeness and demanded to make her presentation and to be listened to. It was hard not to cheer. From that moment on, this member took the floor much more often and became a leader within the group.

Not all the roles were assigned; in another group, a self-confident woman volunteered to be chief negotiator. Faced with the same kinds of employer antics, however, she had to leave the room before bursting into tears. Her team came back to the table without her, and another member took on the chief negotiator role and made a forceful presentation, without preparation.

PARTICIPANT FEEDBACK

After the first year of the program, an outside facilitator held a focus group with participants to evaluate the program, assess the level of commitment to pursue leadership within ETFO and gain insight into if or how lives had changed as a result of participation in L4T. In describing where participants came from, the outside facilitator wrote:

> Many of these women face ongoing oppression. One woman described the discomfort she has experienced within her local as "standing on a rock with sharks around me." In addition, a few of them live in environments where they are physically isolated and have little support among like-minded peers. At times, these circumstances have weakened or inhibited their desire to fight for equity and social justice. (Fournier 2005: 1)

Participants' response to the course was overwhelmingly positive. One woman wrote:

> The world of the marginalized woman within ETFO is not an easy one, and that of those who seek leadership positions is even more challenging. Participants appreciated that the course was reality based. There was no sugar coating. It showed real life situations and how to deal with them. (Fournier 2005: 2)

Two suggestions for improvement were learning about identity and oppression in the first session and providing an early opportunity to articulate individual motivation and intention in choosing L4T, and we made both these changes in subsequent years. Several participants had plans to increase their involvement in ETFO, and while some had been encouraged by local leaders to do so, others reported being actively discouraged or shunned by local leaders.

In the second year of the program (2005–06), ETFO staff working with the L4T program received the following notes from course participants:

> I saw leadership as something to resist.

> For the last ten years, I've been brewing this leadership inside me, and not knowing where to go with it.

> From Day One in the opening circle, when women who were complete strangers to each other started to share intimate thoughts and feelings, I knew I was rapidly being drawn into something very special. When I recall those brief, shy introductions and relate them to the women I now know, I am completely in awe of how much we all grew. This is part of the magic of Leaders; it isn't simply an individual's journey, but rather the growth of the collective. As a group, we encouraged, helped, cajoled and sometimes dragged each other kicking and screaming forward towards new and increasingly lofty goals.

> Whereas one year ago, I would have stated emphatically that I would never run for a local released position, that door now stands slightly ajar.

THE EVOLUTION OF L4T, 2010–14

L4T participants have always provided positive evaluations of the program. After two successful years of L4T, ETFO created another year-long, multisession leadership program that is open to men and women. This Union School first ran in 2006–07, and its design benefited from the experiences with L4T.

With greater staff resources and larger groups of participants, Union School came to be regarded as a signature ETFO leadership program, while L4T became less prominent. L4T participants began to report that the training they received was seen locally as a threat rather than an asset and, in fact, constituted another barrier to acceptance and access to local leadership positions.

For the first six years, a diverse group of three or four women staff members ran the L4T program collaboratively. We included women who designed the program and remained involved over the first six years, while others were staff members who moved in and out of EWS. From 2010 to 2014, the staffing model changed so that a single staff person, a racialized woman, carried responsibility for the course.

Faced with these new realities, the focus of L4T gradually shifted away from union leadership to more broadly based or transferable leadership training. More sessions were held within the work day to accommodate participants' family responsibilities, and social interactions were largely optional. The course focus broadened to include leadership in the teaching profession. Sessions on the community, resume writing and interviewing were introduced. The annual reunion was discontinued, partly due to the large numbers of graduates after the program's fifth year, and, instead, a new program called Next Steps gathered smaller groups of L4T graduates for various optional leadership training experiences such as presentation skills.

L4T GRADUATES

L4T deliberately nurtured a strong group identity among participants and intentionally forged links between the different cohorts through mentoring programs and regular reunions. Our intent was to provide a support group for women who went on to pursue elected leadership positions in the union, in an effort to prevent situations where a member of an equality-seeking group elected to the local or provincial executive would find herself isolated and unable to move her agenda forward. Typically, after one frustrating term in office, these members would choose to put their energies elsewhere. L4T participants were encouraged to work together and strategize around elections and other goals.

Over the years, three L4T graduates have been elected to the provincial executive of ETFO (two were re-elected for a second term) and others elected to local executives. In spring 2015, four members of ETFO's largest local were L4T graduates, and as of 2018, three have been hired to the ETFO provincial staff.[5] Many others exercise their leadership in education as workshop presenters and/or curriculum writers, and some have chosen to become school administrators, leaving the union.

EFTO'S WOMEN'S PROGRAM REVIEW

In 2013–14, ETFO undertook a global review of its programs for women. Morna Ballantyne facilitated focus groups with women graduates of ETFO leadership programs, including L4T. The following are excerpts from Ballantyne's (2014: 3–4, 6) report:

> Most of the participants who now hold union positions said they did so as a direct result of their participation. Leaders for Tomorrow gave focus group participants: confidence to speak out, and take risks; motivation to seek opportunities for advancement; connection with other women teachers and to ETFO; practical skills including the capacity to express ideas verbally and in writing; knowledge about a broad range of subjects, including the education system, politics, and social justice; analysis and understanding complex issues, including racism, discrimination, and the multiple forms of oppression that designated groups face....
>
> Several ... reported that they faced backlash for participating in the ETFO women's program. Even those that did not experience backlash themselves perceived that some members (and some union leaders) are critical of the women's program. There were mixed opinions about how widespread the problem is but some of the women ... reported significant hostility from both male and female coworkers, including accusations of favouritism and/or taking advantage of so-called "reverse discrimination." Some ... reported that their opponents used their participation in the program against them in contested elections. Clearly there is a serious lack of knowledge and understanding ... about systemic discrimination and the importance of affirmative action and/or equity programs in addressing inequality....
>
> The other problem identified by the focus groups was the lack of a leadership path for graduates of ETFO's women's programs. Many ... said that while they learned a great deal through the program, they have had difficulties finding opportunities to apply what they learned. ... They lamented the absence of more female mentors and support systems for those who participated in the program and want to move into leadership positions.

Members discussed other barriers to participation, including the tendency of incumbents to stay in their positions, the reluctance of many women to run against an incumbent, the all-consuming nature of union leadership, the tendency for men to be perceived as natural leaders and a resistance in ETFO's existing leadership to new voices, new faces and new ideas. Ballantyne (2014: 11) concluded:

One of the greatest challenges for the women's programs of all unions is to do more than educate and empower a relatively small number of select women. In order for the education to translate into concrete results, it must be part of a much broader program of change.

FUTURE DIRECTIONS FOR L4T AND FOR ETFO'S WOMEN'S PROGRAMS

The focus group findings informed ETFO's review of its entire women's program offerings. Between 2013 and 2015, staff members worked on establishing common goals and identifying a trajectory of programs from entry level to advanced leadership involvement. The newly established goals of ETFO's women's programs are: 1) to promote women's leadership within ETFO; 2) to outreach specifically to women from designated groups and eliminate barriers to leadership in ETFO; 3) to provide programs that support ETFO women members in both their professional and personal lives; 4) to mobilize women members in becoming social justice and equity activists through professional learning and union leadership development, within the broader community and labour movement; and 5) to support women members in identifying with, and being invested in, their profession and union.

The findings of the focus groups made visible a lack of follow-up for members in ETFO's women's leadership programs, and the entire roster of women's programs was reviewed to identify entry-level, mid-level and advanced-level offerings. Additionally, in 2015–16 ETFO introduced two new advanced programs that provide formal mentoring for women. One of the mentoring programs focused specifically on collective bargaining but is no longer offered. The other, entitled the ETFO Mentor Coaching Institute for Women, is a three-year initiative which used the first year to train women mentors. They were then paired with mentees and spent the following two years together. These women have become a formidable strength within ETFO.

Since 2013, ETFO has placed renewed emphasis on its own employment equity plan in hiring, and the diversity of executive staff has improved. Following a resolution from the 2013 annual meeting, ETFO hired an Indigenous woman member, who was a graduate of L4T and Union School, to carry out responsibilities for FNMI education issues and member engagement. Women now occupy the five most senior administrative roles in the union: the general secretary, two deputy general secretaries, chief financial officer and human resources officer. In addition, all five coordinators of ETFO departments, including collective bargaining, are women.

L4T itself is currently refocused on union leadership and staffed by a diverse organizing committee of ETFO women staff members from all departments. A new expectation is that participants complete a practicum that encourages them to engage at the local level in leadership development and/or addressing a social justice/equity issue. The participants present the results of their practicum at the end of the course.

TRANSFORMATIONS

Many of the women found their L4T experiences to be transformative, both personally and in relation to their participation in the union. Every one of these women came already equipped with impressive skills as educators and with curiosity about their union. While they gained new skills and honed others, the transformations were not really about skill sets. These women found a place within the union where women's experiences were central and valued, where they were encouraged to form lasting and supportive relationships with each other and where questions about how things really (no, really) work were welcomed and answered.

Disappointingly, ETFO itself has not been transformed by L4T; women are still under-represented in leadership roles. As long as this is true, programs like L4T are needed to help women imagine ourselves in positions where we do not see women now. This is not about any deficits of skill, ambition, personal qualities or political instincts among women; ETFO's structures, processes and culture produce the results we see. In this, our union is no different from any other institution in our society, but ETFO explicitly aspires to greater representation of women and members of designated groups. Ongoing discussions within the union, at local and provincial levels, may yet result in needed transformations.

L4T itself continues to evolve, responding to the changing political needs of the union and the cycles of progress, resistance, backlash and resilience that affect social justice and equity work. The women who participated in L4T, both staff and members, have poured their time, intelligence, hearts and creativity into growing progressive women leaders for ETFO and the labour movement.[6]

Notes

1. Other unions represent public secondary teachers, teachers in the province's separate Catholic system and teachers in the French-language system. The four teacher unions all belong to an umbrella organization, the Ontario Teachers' Federation.
2. ETFO Constitution, Article 3.4.
3. Report to the Annual Meeting, August 2004. <etfo.ca/AboutETFO/ProvincialOffice/EquityandWomensServices/Documents/EWS%20Annual%20Report%202004.pdf>. In 2015, 55 percent of local presidents and 56 percent of local chief negotiators were women.

4. Over the years, an average of 9 percent of L4T participants have self-identified as Indigenous, 11 percent self-identified as disabled, 25 percent as lesbian/bisexual and 60 percent as members of racialized groups.

5. In two focus groups of thirty women ETFO members, twenty-eight of whom were L4T graduates, participants held the following union positions (some hold multiple positions): released local executive officer (two); local executive member (five); secretary (one); provincial committee chair (one); regional council member (two); steward or alternate steward (six); local committee chair (six); and local committee member (five). Thirteen of thirty (43 percent) of focus group participants did not hold a union position (Ballantyne 2014).

6. Carol Zavitz is now retired from ETFO and was involved in developing and running L4T for its first six years. Carol Zavitz thanks Kathleen Loftus, Sherry Ramrattan-Smith, Jan Beaver, Kalpana Makan, Jacqueline Karsemeyer, Belinda Longe, Kelly Hayes, Rachel Mishenene, Pam Dogra, Erin Orida, Kate Sharpe, Jeanie Nishimura, Morna Ballantyne, Sharon O'Halloran and Victoria Réaume.

CHAPTER NINE

WOMEN BREAKING BARRIERS
Using Education to Develop
Women's Leadership Inside Canada's Largest Union

Morna Ballantyne and Jane Stinson

In 2005, the Canadian Union of Public Employees (CUPE) launched a new education program under the banner: Women Breaking Barriers. CUPE is Canada's largest national union, representing workers across the country who are employed in a wide array of jobs in a broad range of public services in municipalities, health care, education, social services and other sectors. The Women Breaking Barriers (WBB) program was special for several reasons. First, it was open only to women members. Second, CUPE National took the unusual step of covering the full costs of participation, rather than making local unions pay, and consequently decided who would participate. Third, the union applied program admission criteria to ensure a diverse group of participants with respect to race, age and life experience. Fourth, the purpose of the program was to encourage more women to run for election as CUPE leaders at the local, provincial, sector, and national levels.

We begin by analyzing the context and conditions that gave rise to the WBB education program, then we explain the goals of the WBB course, the participant selection process and the curriculum covered in this five-day, in-residence union education program. We share the views of women who participated in the first year of the course: what stood out for them, what they found most valuable and whether the course changed their roles in the union and their views of union leadership. We conclude the chapter by discussing the transformational learning experienced by course participants and the organizational changes needed to support women union leaders.

Our perspectives and analysis are rooted in and shaped by our own experiences as two union educators, long-time feminist activists and national CUPE staff members who developed the Women Breaking Barriers course, delivered it on a number of occasions, learned from the participants and are now retired from CUPE. We reviewed the literature about women's union leadership development and union education to situate this case study of a women's leadership program within the related literature. We did not find any recent, Canadian studies on the role and importance of union education to women's leadership in our literature review, a significant gap this book seeks to fill. An earlier study, however, did show how union education programs designed by and for women played a key role in politicizing women and helping women learn how to advocate inside unions to advance women's concerns (Briskin 1999).

IMPORTANCE OF UNION EDUCATION IN WOMEN'S LEADERSHIP

Linda Briskin's research shows that union education in Canada, by and for women, contributes to change by providing the following:

- an opportunity to critically analyze patriarchal practices in unions and workplaces, which function to exclude women and other marginalized groups;
- a space for women to develop their distinct voice and identity; and
- a strategic means of transforming the culture and structure of unions.

Historically, women's union courses, designed by and for women, served to strengthen the demands of women workers, including expanded maternity benefits, marriage law reform and equal pension rights. Briskin argues that the approach and educational methods used in courses organized by and for women can have a transformative impact. The experience encourages women to adopt different practices as union activists and leaders — to be more inclusive and informal in meetings, listen more and be less bureaucratic and hierarchical. This theory of the power of women's union education is consistent with our personal experiences as union educators, and it informed the development of the WBB course.

For this book chapter, we conducted primary research in two ways: through document analysis of the original WBB course proposal and goals, discussed and approved by the CUPE National Executive Board, and the original five-day course curriculum. We also surveyed a hundred women who took the first WBB course, mailing them a description of our research goals and inviting them to share their views through a web-based survey of twenty-four questions. Thirteen requests to participate in the survey were returned unopened. However, eleven women responded — a high number (almost 13 percent of the women we reached) considering that more than ten years had passed since they participated in the program. The responses provided rich, qualitative data.

ORIGINS OF WOMEN BREAKING BARRIERS

CUPE is Canada's largest trade union, with a reported membership of 630,000 workers organized into 2,400 local unions spread across the country (CUPE 2014). Women make up 68 percent of CUPE's membership (CUPE 2015). CUPE locals have high expectations of their national union and take an active interest in its governance. More than a thousand delegates from CUPE local unions attend the CUPE national convention, held every two years, to set national policies and plans and to elect two full-time officers, a national president and national secretary-treasurer, as well as members of the National Executive Committee.

The 2003 national convention opened a new chapter in CUPE's history. Judy Darcy, who was national secretary-treasurer (1989–91) and then national president for the next twelve years, announced in early 2003 that she would step down as president. Geraldine McGuire, the female national secretary-treasurer elected with Darcy in 1991, had retired two years earlier. Other changes at the provincial level created many vacancies on the National Executive Board that year. Convention delegates audibly gasped when they first saw the seven, newly elected male members of the National Executive Committee face them at the front of the convention to take their oath of office.[1] Delegates suddenly seemed to realize that they had elected only (white) men as the union's national leadership. "Where are the women?" one delegate called out, and others yelled similar sentiments.

The absence of women on the National Executive Committee, and the election of only six women to twenty-three positions on the full National Executive Board, made visible a long-standing problem in CUPE. Until 2003, a woman had held the position of national president for most of CUPE's history,[2] but the number of women on the National Executive Board was never proportionate to the number of women in CUPE. Women's committees complained of being marginalized and under-funded at both the provincial and national levels. Racialized women, Indigenous women, lesbian women and women with disabilities were particularly vocal about the lack of progress on their concerns, including representation on the union's top decision-making bodies.

Mounting discontent with the status quo spurred women delegates at the 2003 national convention to organize a women's caucus for the first time in many years and to take to the microphones in an organized way to argue for change. This, and a strategic directions policy paper adopted at that convention that called on CUPE to make equality rights central to the work of the union, propelled the male-dominated national leadership to take action. After consultation with the CUPE National Women's Committee, and further debates at CUPE provincial conventions through the spring of 2004, the National Executive Board gave the green light to a number of initiatives, including the creation of a new educational program for emerging women leaders called Women Breaking Barriers.

WHO PARTICIPATED IN WOMEN BREAKING BARRIERS?

Women were selected for the course based on a new application process giving preference to applicants who met the following criteria:

- significant union experience in their local union, provincial division or other CUPE structures including district councils and/or sector councils/committees;
- basic knowledge and understanding of CUPE and labour relations;
- past or present involvement in social justice organizations or causes;
- demonstrated desire for more knowledge and skills to assume greater leadership responsibilities in CUPE; and
- no plan to retire in the near future.

It was difficult to identify who in CUPE might be a potential female candidate for a senior elected position nationally, provincially or in a particular sector, and who might therefore benefit from a national leadership program. The first challenge was to ensure that the call for female course candidates reached deeply and evenly into the union. The new five-day course was advertised widely, with a notice sent to all local unions and staff, posted on CUPE websites and distributed at union events, including conferences and schools. Despite the advertising, the response rate was low, with approximately two applicants for every one of the available hundred spaces. Almost all were women who had been encouraged to apply by the CUPE education staff or CUPE staff service representatives and who had attended other education workshops and union events.

Most of the applicants were actively recruited because they were considered by staff to be leadership material. This approach to selecting members for union events or activities is not unusual. Union members are often "tapped" for leadership opportunities. The difficulty is that members not known to staff or others in positions of influence can be missed, even if they meet selection criteria. In CUPE, women tend to lead the small to mid-size union locals that are more predominantly female. However, these local women leaders are at a disadvantage when it comes to participating in activities outside of their local and demonstrating to others, including those responsible for education programs, their interest and ability to assume greater leadership roles. This is because the smaller to mid-size locals tend to represent the lowest paid workers and therefore have a smaller dues-base, making it difficult to fund much beyond direct member representation, such as negotiations and grievance arbitrations.

A second issue was the difficulty women faced in getting away for six to seven days (including travel time) to attend an in-residence course. Household and family responsibilities were insurmountable barriers for some women. Others were unable to get time off work because their collective agreement provisions could not stop the employer from denying them union leave. These are examples of systemic barriers to women's full participation in union education and other union activities. Fortunately, CUPE's National Executive Board removed the financial bar to participation by fully funding each participant with national union funds. Women received additional funds for family-related costs. Even with that support, three participants had to leave before the course ended in order to attend to family-related emergencies.

By paying the full costs of the program, CUPE National was able to determine the process and criteria to select participants and set standards for staying in the program. The course facilitators closely monitored participants' engagement in the learning process and had the authority to address problems. This was unusual in CUPE because, at least at that time, the conduct of participants at union schools was normally left to local unions to address since they chose the course participants and paid most of the costs.[3]

To be considered to attend a WBB course, applicants needed the endorsement of their local president for both practical and political reasons. Practically, requests for union leave to attend union events normally must be submitted to the employer by the local president or local executive. Politically, local leadership support was needed so that women returning from the course could get local support to act on their leadership aspirations and put their new knowledge to work. It is impossible to say if some women were excluded from applying because they could not get their local president's signature on the application form. While no official complaints were filed, some participants, during the course, noted that some members of their local executive viewed the WBB program negatively, complaining that women were being given a training opportunity not available to men and that this would give women an advantage in local union elections.

The provincial/regional education staff received and reviewed the applications and recommended qualified candidates to the national director of union development. Through discussion, a final list was developed and shared with the provincial division presidents, who were invited to provide additional comments about the candidates. Final selection of the candidates considered race, Indigenous status, disabilities and sexual orientation as well as geography, occupation and sector to ensure diversity among the course cohorts. The five-day WBB course was offered three times between September and November 2005, first in British Columbia for women from that province and Alberta (twenty-five participants), then in Nova Scotia for women from the Atlantic region (twenty-six participants), and finally in Ontario (twenty-six participants). A smaller fourth group of eleven Manitoba women took the course in the early summer of 2006 as part of a regularly scheduled week-long CUPE school. The leadership of the Quebec and Saskatchewan Divisions of CUPE, in consultation with the education staff from those provinces, opted not to participate in the program, preferring instead to give women activists in their provinces access to courses they had developed outside of the national education program.

DESIGN OF THE WBB COURSE

The following assumptions guided the design of CUPE's WBB course:

- Women's inequality in CUPE cannot be addressed without the following: 1) understanding the dialectical relationship between the situation of women in the union and the position of women in the context of global capitalism and patriarchy, and 2) changing social, political and legal structures and institutions;
- Changing the status of women in unions requires addressing systemic barriers, particularly those rooted in the material conditions of women. It also requires a shift in power relations. Tackling ideas and attitudes by educating people to think differently is not the solution, although it can help to create momentum and support for underlying systemic change;
- A structural deficit is the main barrier to women reaching high-level positions in unions, not a personal skills deficit. In CUPE, many women serve on their local union executives, including many in the position of president.[4] Many women have significant union experience and skills at a local level, as well as formal education beyond high school. The barriers to women taking on provincial and national leadership run much deeper than simply having equal skills to run for leadership positions; and,
- Women who serve in top leadership roles in unions can play an important role in advancing women's equality (or broader equality rights), but they do not do so just because they are women. In order to successfully advance women's equality, women union leaders must choose (or be pressured) to take deliberate action, first and foremost by organizing with other women, but also with male allies.

Formal union policy didn't articulate these points of view, nor were they widely held by CUPE activists. In fact, the dominant thinking at the time was that women and men are equal and to say otherwise is demeaning to women. Women delegates to provincial and national CUPE conventions would frequently say to thunderous applause during debates on resolutions calling for affirmative action measures that women don't need "special treatment"

— that they prefer to be elected on their own merits. This line was delivered again at the subsequent 2007 national convention debate on a proposal to create two new full-time national positions designated for women (Hall 2007).

In this context, the WBB course offered a radical analysis of the situation of women and fostered discussion of far-reaching solutions. It gave participants an opportunity to identify the root causes, effects and manifestation of women's oppression by exploring their own life experiences in their families, communities, workplaces and in CUPE. The course offered women a theoretical framework to make sense of their experiences of inequality and to start formulating the elements of a comprehensive program for change: one that touched on transforming systems and institutions, including the union. The course also included skills-building modules to give participants hands-on tools for moving change forward, as well as confidence to use the tools when they returned home. Finally, and importantly, the course was designed to build ongoing solidarity and sisterhood to support participants in their continued union work. In this way, the course addressed, in theory and practice, the role of women's networks or caucuses in making feminist change.

CURRICULUM HIGHLIGHTS

The status of women was examined through participants' own experiences in their workplaces, communities, homes and union. Participants analyzed each of these spheres of life, and the connections between them, through a series of participatory "mapping" activities. Women experienced poignant moments of discovery related to how much time they, relative to men, spend caring for others in their jobs, in the community and at home. They probed the extent to which this caring work is undervalued and undercompensated by employers and their own union and society as a whole.

The Women Breaking Barriers curriculum was based on a spiral model of learning that builds on participants' experiences and knowledge. It assumed that:

- workers in labour education are not empty vessels waiting for an instructor to fill them;
- learning is about making sense of experiences and the world we live in, making connections between individual and collective experiences, and adding new information to what we already know;
- union activists learn best through active participation; and
- union learning should prepare participants to further their union engagement and take action on the issues addressed through the learning process.

The Triangle Tool for examining systems of oppression (Burke,

Geronimo, Martin, Thomas and Wall 2002) was adapted to explore what underlies individual and dominant collective behaviour and beliefs about women's equality. The Triangle Tool (referred to in the course as the "iceberg model for understanding oppression") helped clarify the role institutions and systems play in shaping ideas and behaviour, and the dialectical relationship between individuals, systems and institutions. This analytical framework served as the entry point for an analysis of the workings of the capitalist economy, as experienced by the participants, and to an examination of two institutions: the media and unions.

Discussion of how not all women experience oppression in the same way, and not all women experience the same oppressions, wove the theory and practice of intersectional feminism throughout the course. Participants found these discussions challenging at times, particularly with respect to white privilege, made more difficult because most participants and facilitators were white. Participants were introduced, most for the first time, to three theories advanced but seldom named outside of academic courses, to explain women's inequality: biological determinism, liberal idealism and historical material-ism. This discussion challenged the prevailing view in many unions that the main obstacles to women's equality are people's attitudes and women's lack of confidence and/or training.

Early in the five-day curriculum, male leaders in elected and staff posi-tions were invited to a question-and-answer forum with the women to explain the (predominantly male) path to provincial, national and staff leadership positions in CUPE. An interesting dynamic emerged here: the women, perhaps empowered by their discussions and new learning in the course, posed chal-lenging questions, which, as they shared during the debriefing, they would never have had the courage to ask in another setting. Some of the male leaders commented later to the facilitators that this forum caused them to reflect in a more conscious or deliberate way on their own rise to leadership and to recognize their own privilege.

Through activities and tools, participants examined how the institutional behaviour of unions, as opposed to the individual behaviour of union mem-bers, created barriers to women's participation. This structural analysis of unions generated an array of suggestions on how union work, and labour relations generally, could be done differently to be more inclusive of women and other traditionally excluded groups.

Several components of the curriculum developed participants' skills. One was a participatory theatre exercise inspired by Brazilian educator Paulo Freire (2000) and dramatist Augusto Boal (2000) that explored sexism in the workplace and union. All participants were encouraged to take the role of the harassed woman in a skit to practise how to deal with sexist behaviours. As well, mobilization training, public speaking and research exercises were integrated into the program throughout the week. Participants had many opportunities to analyze union challenges and practise articulating their views as leaders in a variety of forms, including short speeches, debates and in writing during the course.

PARTICIPANTS' FEEDBACK ABOUT THE COURSE

Ten years later, eleven women who participated in the first series of five-day WBB courses offered across the country provided insights into their experience through our survey. Four women were from the Atlantic region course, three were from Ontario, one from the Manitoba session and one from the combined British Columbia and Alberta session. Two survey participants did not identify where they took the course. Women who took the course ranged from 30 to 55 years of age at the time. Seven of the eleven women were responsible for children and/or parents at the time of the course, six of the eleven women had a partner at the time of the course, two more had divorced or were in the process of divorcing, and three had no partner.

All eleven women had been elected to local union officer positions, and some were elected or appointed to provincial and national committees, at the time they took the WBB course. Six of the eleven women were still active in CUPE when they answered the survey, and most had been elected to higher leadership positions than ten years earlier when they took the course. The other five women reported they are no longer active in CUPE for a variety of reasons, including retirement, leaving employment represented by CUPE, being bullied out of their local position and stepping down for personal reasons such as helping care for a father diagnosed with Alzheimer's disease.

Most of the women reported they took the WBB course to learn more about the union and their role in it, and about women's issues in the labour movement. Some wanted to gain confidence, both generally and in specific areas, such as public speaking. Some were frustrated by the absence of elected women leaders, especially in the national leadership, and others wanted to connect and network with other women in the union.

Most women (seven) said gaining confidence was the greatest benefit from the course, followed by public speaking skills (five) and listening and developing more patience (two).

> Speaking to a group [was one thing I learned]. Confidence in my role in the union. Helped me see the bigger picture! I was influenced by my sister members to keep up the fight! I no longer mind asking questions, and I don't just take what the powers that be or the media have to say as fact.... I learned how things get manipulated for the good of those in power. I learned that women are a very, very strong part of our union and I am proud of the work we do!

> The biggest challenge I faced as a woman leader was my lack of self-confidence. I did not think I was smart enough or good enough to do the job. The course gave me the confidence and introduced me to women that I could turn to for support.

Women identified a number of other specific benefits from the course. The number in parentheses after the benefit is the number of women who responded to that benefit.

- It deepened my understanding of women's position in society (8).
- It built my confidence (8).
- It gave me practical suggestions for improving things for women at work (7).
- It gave me a better understanding of my role in the union (7).
- It provided me with opportunity to network (6).
- It gave me a better understanding of how the union works (5).

Additionally, women provided the following feedback: the group activities were a great confidence builder and very informative; the public-speaking activity was hard but great; and the information portion of the course was invaluable, including exercises dealing with facts versus myths, the distribution of wealth and how to respond to the media. The course also prompted them to rethink assumptions about themselves as women. One woman said: "[We were] challenged to assess our personal lives and look beyond the reasons we normally give for the division of labour at home." Some women reported the course helped them find new ways to balance work and family.

Learning more about the economy was another important course goal. Women said they learned about power and wealth, growing inequality and its disproportionate impact on women, and that "a right-wing economic agenda devalues people" while "a strong public service work force creates a strong economy."

> For me the part of the course that often comes to mind in my union involvement was the economic discussions. How the economic inequality has a greater impact on women.

The course confirmed their experiences, at the time of the course, that while women needed to work extra hard in an economy where wages were not fair, they also believed that "our union holds power and we can affect change." Many of the women said they learned about the gains that women had won, but also that much still needed to be done. They said they learned that:

- women's inequality is pervasive in society;

- women's inequality is driven by capitalism and is preventable;
- home responsibilities prevent many great women from becoming union leaders; and
- structural changes like designated seats on union executive bodies are needed for women, given patriarchy and the historical assignment of positions based on gender.

One participant added the following:

> The Women Breaking Barriers workshop made me feel more comfortable and competent in addressing inequality. After the workshop, I spoke up more in situations where I felt there was something that needed to be addressed. In repeating some of the questions that were asked of me that week, I was able to encourage others to more deeply assess some familiar practices, mechanisms, behaviours, et cetera that we were part of.

In response to an open-ended question about what they learned about making political change, six women indicated they learned to consider others' opinions and to question statements. Other comments were that "politics is involved in everything," that women have a lot to offer, that structural change is needed to make political change in CUPE, specifically seats designated for women on the National Executive Board and that one voice or one local can make a difference. As well, a few women mentioned that it was important not to be put off by those who don't see inequality and not let them stop change. One woman commented:

> I learned that it is only through engaging with people who have contradictory views that we can be part of real change. We should not be put off or discouraged by those who refuse to see inequality. We should not ignore or discount contradictory views. In the end, however, if consensus cannot be reached or common ground cannot be found, people who refuse to acknowledge inequality should not be allowed to prevent what needs to be said or done.

WOMEN'S UNION LEADERSHIP

The survey responses show that the WBB course shifted what the participants thought about union leadership. They saw new ways of being union leaders — to use consensus rather than follow a leader, to rely on others and to be a good listener. A few learned that leadership is not necessarily defined by position; they realized they could be a leader at any position or role in the union. Some said they learned about the responsibilities of being a leader and the need for more women's voices in CUPE and the broader labour movement.

> A union leader does not always have to have a title and all the responsibilities that go with it. You can lead in whatever capacity you can commit to until you have the knowledge, confidence and ability to do more. As a leader we must look to encourage and enable all members to be able to do whatever they can for their local.

These women said that giving and receiving support and working together to assume leadership were the most important things they learned about becoming a woman union leader. They indicated support for a gendered or feminist model of leadership that recognized leadership is not about a single leader who makes all of the decisions. In this shared leadership model, women valued working together, building on each other's strengths, asking others for help, mentoring others, recognizing everyone has a part to play in the union and seeing the need to support each other.

Most of the women who responded said that after taking the WBB course they ran for and were elected to positions from local union president to regional vice-president on the National Executive Board. Almost half of the women who responded said they had had no or few obstacles in achieving and fulfilling their leadership roles, but half of the women who responded noted problems. Women most frequently raised family and home responsibilities as their biggest barrier on their leadership path after the WBB course. Three women raised how difficult it was to juggle all the responsibilities when in leadership positions, including those in the home and trying to also have a personal life. One woman cited caring for elderly parents as the reason she stepped down from a provincial elected position that took her around the province. For another it was life's challenges:

> Life. I was three years single and during that time had a very challenging time with family issues (children). I was stretched to the max with responsibilities at home and the union had to be put on the back burner for a while. Having said that my local was always supportive. We have a small but mighty union of nine women!

Half of the women said their greatest challenge once elected was negativity toward them as women leaders. This included put-downs by management:

> The most challenging thing I found was making male employers take me seriously rather than try to undermine my leadership with the rest of my membership.

Others cited competition, lack of support from women and male-dominated locals not wanting to hear about inequality.

> I think the most challenging part about being a women leader for me is the negativity. My most challenging task is staying confident with so much competition and lack of support from other women. Strong supportive women are the reason I wanted to continue working in the labour movement but I do not have the same support now with so many retirements and I guess the position I am in, and I miss it.

A few women identified gender-based opposition from others in the union as a problem, such as a participant who was opposed as a leader on the grounds that she would represent only women's interests and because she was a single parent with two kids. Others named challenges such as "understanding the organization and what the barriers are" and that there is "a different expectation from women than men and we need to change perceptions."

Women stated what they gained from the course that helped them meet challenges as women leaders. These included greater confidence, assertiveness and finding their voice to speak up and question things; and support and strength from other women by recognizing others had similar experiences and by introducing them to other women they could turn to for support.

Women's comments throughout the survey indicated that they found the course extremely or very important in developing them as a leader in CUPE.

> I found this course was a major turning point in my leadership path. Up until I took this program I did not feel confident in myself and my own abilities. Even after retirement I have taken on positions at the local political level.

IMPORTANCE OF A WOMEN-ONLY COURSE

In the survey all of the women spoke to the importance of WBB as a women-only course. All raised advantages of only having women present. They said it contributed to women being more relaxed and that there was more sharing, bonding, expression of feelings and open communication than there would have been if men had been present. Women felt that men's presence "changes the atmosphere," that men "use male privilege to dominate," that "some women defer to them [men]" and that women who have experienced sexual abuse and harassment are more relaxed and open when men are not present. Women also felt men need to prove themselves more and have trouble being honest about their insecurities.

> We are wired differently. We express our feelings differently. We were able after a day or so to really talk about things openly without having to prove we "can do it all." I think it would have taken longer to let

your guard down in mixed company. I love my CUPE brothers but it sometimes takes a while for them to let their guard down in front of other brothers (especially) and sisters. Most important, the men would not have enjoyed our Dollar Store CUPE Spa night. LOL.

I felt more at ease with women only. It has been my experience that in a co-ed setting men tend to dominate group discussions, and I was really interested in hearing and understanding the content of the program from a female perspective.

The views of the women were consistent with research cited earlier that found women-only union courses provide a unique learning environment that can increase women's participation and activism and advance gender equality within the union more than mixed-sex courses. One reason may be that women-only courses encourage and help participants to identify with women as an oppressed or disadvantaged social group within union structures, whether or not disadvantage is personally experienced. As well, women-only courses often encourage participants to take part in collective action with the aim of seeking to overcome women's inequality in the workplace and the union (Green and Kirton 2002). Others have pointed to the importance of women-only educational forums in creating a comfortable learning environment for women (Raposo, Robinson, Kelly and Grant 2003).

It is significant to consider what happened when one of the women-only WBB courses was held as part of a regular, mixed-gender, in-residence union school rather than on its own. At this school, a group of male students (identified by some as biker-like because they wore leather and rode motorcycles) set up an informal "party central" in their adjoining rooms. The party started soon after the end of each day's classes, significant amounts of alcohol were consumed, and the music played loudly well into the night. Some women raised this situation in discussions in the WBB course as an example of behaviour at union activities that made them uncomfortable and served to marginalize them. When the school organizers intervened to address the matter, tensions mounted between the WBB participants and some of the students in the regular, mixed-gender union school.

Another point of conflict surfaced over the presence of children at the school. Although on-site childcare was routinely offered at union schools, few students ever brought children. However, since special efforts were made to ensure that women with children would be able to attend the WBB course, more children than usual were registered and were therefore present at mealtimes. Some female participants from other workshops complained that the children were diminishing their school experience and the benefits of having time away from their own children.

Women's learning in the WBB course was affected by these out-of-classroom issues that, on the one hand, provided important real-life subject matter for discussion and learning. On the other hand, the WBB participants were frustrated that addressing these problems took time away from the planned curriculum. They felt that the school environment negatively affected their overall learning experience. The facilitators also noted that there was less bonding between the course participants at the WBB course offered in conjunction with the mixed-gender school than there was between those who participated in the stand-alone WBB courses. One woman noted that at the independent WBB sessions, "the environment we were in — isolated — contributed to the learning experience.... The emotional work we had had to do was difficult but watching others work though their struggles made it easier." Women got together socially in small and large groups at night. At one session, the participants spent free time together treating themselves well (doing their hair, manicures, going to the spa), shopping together (often for their family) and they danced as a large group of women at the local bar.

TRANSFORMATIONAL LEARNING

The Women Breaking Barriers course proved to be transformational for the women who participated. At the conclusion of the course, during the evaluation module, participants said they had shifted how they saw their own situation and the world around them, including the economy, their own home life, their position in the union and their view of leadership. This was consistent with Briskin's (2006) research on the transformative impacts of union education organized by and for women. Similar to what happened to women through feminist education and consciousness raising groups in the 1960s and 1970s, the participants in WBB came to realize, through their discussions and analysis, that what they were experiencing in the union individually was also being experienced by others and that both individual and collective action would be required to achieve equality.

Participants also made important connections between the problems they were facing in the workplace with those they were experiencing at home, in their communities and in their union. For many this was a revelation and it contributed to their growing understanding throughout the week that what they were experiencing in all these spheres of life was rooted in both patriarchy and capitalism and perpetuated through institutions like the media, the courts, schools, the legislatures and unions themselves. At the start of the course, some women resisted these ideas. For example, some stated that women who are experiencing problems of poverty or abuse have an individual responsibility to get out of their situation. To assert otherwise, they argued, was to regard women as helpless victims. These participants believed that to say women are oppressed is to say that women are not equal. By the end of the course, some of these women said they had fundamentally changed their view.

The course also transformed how the participants saw themselves as women. They came to understand and acknowledge their true worth in all spheres of their lives. For example, they were able to analyze and put a value on their work at home and in the community. Also, they came to understand and appreciate their skills and the transferability of their skills from one sphere of life to another, such as the applicability of their household management skills to organizing union functions. It is not surprising perhaps that in the survey women identified building confidence as a benefit of the course. While the course taught skills, such as how to craft and deliver a speech, for the most part it helped make the participants' extensive existing skills visible and be affirmed as valuable.

Most participants' views of leadership, particularly union leadership, shifted through the course of the week. In discussions about leadership at the outset of the course, most participants shared the view that union leaders had to be commanding, strong, opinionated, confrontational and charismatic. However, through the course, they learned (from union leadership theory but also through their own practice during the week) the benefits of listening to others and learning from others' experiences before taking positions; involving others in collective leadership by sharing responsibilities rather than assuming individual control; being reflective rather than reactive; and making an effort to develop and sustain a culture of caring and cooperation rather than competition. Two views summed it up:

> It did change my views on what it means to be a union leader. Well, I realized that as a union leader you need to be a good listener as well as a leader.

> It takes courage and I could rely on my sisters. Women work on a consensus model rather than follow the leader.

This approach to leadership, associated in literature with feminist leadership, as well as with transformational leadership (Briskin 2006), is believed by some to be essential to the renewal of trade unions because it is "the most effective leadership approach for organizations facing significant changes and challenges" (Clark 2000: 175).

The survey of participants revealed that the course had a long-term impact on them. They were able to comment in detail on the course content and its effects on them, even ten years after participating. None identified shortcomings with the course content, even in retrospect. There were only a few suggestions for curriculum changes, including more icebreakers at the outset to get people to feel comfortable with each other and adding a session on "how women can support each other" to address the negative impact of jealousy and competition among women union activists.

ORGANIZATIONAL TRANSFORMATION

Although participants in WBB changed through the experience, it is not possible to change a union through one course. Barriers persist for CUPE women, as for women in all unions. For example, survey participants revealed how frequently family responsibilities forced them out of leadership roles or prevented them from pursuing leadership positions. Seven of the women identified the absence of ongoing leadership support for women, including feedback, support, mentoring and continuous training. They noted the need for more opportunities for women to learn from other women and to put in place mechanisms for women to stay in touch after courses such as WBB. The importance of national funding was raised as one of the most important ways to encourage and assist women to become elected leaders in CUPE. Women recognized how hard it is for other women, especially from small locals, to get their local unions to agree to pay for them to attend a five-day course like WBB. The need to fund childcare was also noted.

WBB may have had a more far-reaching impact for participants, and for all CUPE members, had it been part of a broader organizational change initiative. For example, it is difficult to see how the barrier of family responsibilities can be addressed without an organizational shift in how leadership is viewed and supported. Many of the union's internal structural and systemic barriers would likely be lowered if a feminist and transformational model of leadership was embraced by the entire union and supported by budgets, programs and formal constitutional change where required. Women in unions can, and should, lead the organizational change required to create the space needed for women leaders to take their place. However, they need resources to do so, and they need organizational structures and support, such as women's committees, caucuses, more women-only education and other mechanisms that bring women together to decide the change they need and to push for it.

Union women will not succeed by organizing for change in isolation. Unions must start to see the issue of women's leadership as a question of gendered leadership. Women need access to transformational change education like WBB, but so too do men. Leadership cannot only be redefined for women — it must be redefined for men too. This requires radical and profound change with far-reaching consequences. It will help open new doors to the further democratization of unions and increase their power through greater engagement and empowerment of women and other marginalized groups, including the men in these groups. By supporting the development of female and feminist leadership, unions would be in a better position to grow their membership, increase their strength and power, advance greater equality and continue to achieve real gains for members and all workers.

Notes

1. CUPE's National Executive Committee is made up of the national president, national secretary-treasurer and five general vice-presidents, who provide regional representation across the country (one from British Columbia or Alberta, one from Saskatchewan or Manitoba, one from Ontario, one from Quebec and one from one of the Atlantic provinces).
2. Grace Hartman served as CUPE national president from 1975 to 1983, and Judy Darcy from 1991 to 2013.
3. Now participants in union events, including schools and workshops, are expected to conduct themselves according to a code of conduct instituted by CUPE National in 2010. This initiative emerged from a recommendation by a special CUPE National Women's Task Force (2007).
4. In 2005, women made up approximately 66 percent of the CUPE membership and women held the position of president in 48 percent of CUPE locals (CUPE 2005).

CHAPTER TEN

CRITICAL LOVE LETTER TO THE PSUW

Adriane Paavo and Cindy Hanson

The two of us approach the topic of women's labour education from some similar and some different perspectives. We were both born in the early 1960s to working-class settler families in rural Saskatchewan. We became feminists because of *and* in spite of this backdrop. Adriane has worked inside the labour movement since the early 1990s. She is one of the founders of the Prairie School for Union Women (PSUW), serving on the Steering Committee for sixteen years. Cindy's lifelong work with social movements is from both within and outside of the labour movement. She views the work of the school from the perspective of a community activist and an adult educator specializing in non-formal learning. Although we write this letter with a focus on the PSUW, the school we know best, we are very aware that the lessons for other labour schools within our experiences hold true here as well.

From these different connections with the PSUW, we both developed strong feelings for the school: admiration and excitement for its accomplishments and innovations; loyalty and protectiveness for its survival and success; and a longing to be part of its life. What is this if not, in essence, love? Love for the event and for all those who contribute to it. Love is often the emotion that guides activism. For example, Che Guevara, bell hooks (2003) and Paulo Freire (1997) all speak of the need for love to guide the work of activists. Such love motivated our commitment to carry out two studies about the school (described in Chapter 2), to create this book and finally to write these reflections in our own voices.

This chapter does not pretend to be from the head. It is from our hearts. It was important for us to write this love letter to provoke critical thinking about feminist labour education and organizing. We wanted to raise questions useful to organizers of future feminist labour education projects, particularly about the way that bureaucratization can creep into movements.

WHY ARE WE DOING THIS WORK?

Adriane: I was quite new to working in the labour movement when the call came for women to gather and talk about creating a women-only labour school in Saskatchewan. I went along because it was an interesting idea and because lots of senior activists and leaders I admired were taking part. But I was quickly convinced of the school's potential for strengthening women's leadership and activism.

The moment it really hit me that we were on to something special was the first day of the 1999 school. I ran into a woman, the president of one of the locals I serviced, who was attending for the first time. She had a really strange look on her face, and I asked her what was the matter. She said: "This is the first time in fifteen years I've been away from home without either my husband or one of my kids." She wasn't scared or lonely; she was giddy with the opportunity to just focus on herself, her own thoughts and needs, for four and a half days.

The Prairie School for Union Women — and other women's labour-education events — create spaces for women to reflect on our lives, our experiences and our needs. We get to talk with women from other communities and unions and find out that we're not alone in what we want and what we face. We hear our own voices. We see others listening to and valuing our words. We get a taste of our own potential. We connect with allies and ideas. This is why I care about the PSUW and other events like it.

Cindy: I first learned about the PSUW from an article in the magazine *Briarpatch* and then from running into a friend who was excited about her opportunity to facilitate at the school. I was active previously in the Co-operative College of Canada and I was a feminist — I had an intuitive activist's sense of the importance of this school. Many years later, when I had the opportunity to undertake the two studies on the PSUW, I was convinced this was an invaluable, non-formal learning experience in the lives of many women. Further, and in part because of my work with the Labour College of Canada, I understood how the PSUW was movement-building — something so necessary in fighting the neoliberal austerity policies that affect all of our lives, but particularly the lives of those economically and socially marginalized. That sense of necessity emerged again in a more recent issue of *Briarpatch* (Kagis and Byers 2017).

WHAT INSIGHTS CAN WE OFFER?

Adriane: Women-only schools are important places to nurture future feminist leaders. There are not many places like this within the labour movement, especially spaces that women completely control. So we have to take these spaces seriously. That means using every aspect of the school, the planning as well as the running of it, as spaces for women to experience and practise their organizational and decision-making skills. No element of the organizing is so trivial or so important that it should not be seen as a venue for learning leadership and gaining confidence.

We did this faithfully in the early years of the Prairie School for Union Women. That is, activities that elsewhere would be planned by union or labour-federation staff, were instead planned by the women who volunteered. This included things like ordering t-shirts and other promotional items, running registration and setting up the childcare. Usually the women who volunteered were rank-and-file sisters. Often, they were sisters for whom this was a first chance to take charge of something outside of their homes and jobs. Sometimes they failed and had to be rescued. Usually they did just fine. We saw a number of women bloom and grow as a result of taking on tasks.

We also had a rule: "three years and rest." That meant that no one could facilitate at the school for more than three years in a row. After a break, they could be asked again. But it forced us to include other women in a powerful leadership role. It forced us to offer regular facilitation courses at the school, so that we were deliberately adding to the pool of choices. This isn't always easy. Every organization faces choices about bureaucratization. So does the PSUW. It's easier and safer to have the same people do things over and over again, because it reduces the risk of problems. Learning is messy and unpredictable. My advice: take the risk. Deliberately put new people in charge of logistics. Deliberately do not invite the same facilitators to do the same courses. Resist the safe, easy route and expand the ranks of those taking action and being the face of the school.

The PSUW continues to be a great laboratory for innovative ideas about labour education. In this respect, it does resist bureaucratization. Because women-only schools and programs are still often seen as *in addition to* regular programming, we may be able to get away with trying out courses, techniques and activities that would not be quite so acceptable in other education venues. The PSUW was and is a space to try out new approaches in childcare provision, in courses on environmentalism or different family structures or art as a venue for social change, and in methods of mentoring emerging facilitators. Innovative ideas sometimes fail, but it is invaluable to have a supportive space to try.

Finally, I'd offer the advice that we acknowledge that our schools are special bubbles and that the outside world is still there and needs to be engaged with. During women-only events, before participants leave, we need to alert them that they may not be using their new confidence, skills and ideas in an environment as supportive as the school was, so that they are not destroyed by that sharp shock of transition. But more importantly, the community of feminist labour educators needs to expand our collective thinking and practice about how to extend the experience and feeling of our schools and programs beyond their time and space, through real and virtual events that reconnect women with one another and with the power and confidence they experienced at the event itself. If our schools are the greenhouse where seeds of new potential take root, then what kinds of gardening practices can we employ to make sure as many seedlings as possible thrive and grow in the tough soil of real life?

Cindy: Feminism is hard work and subject to constant scrutiny. I have been part of a feminist community all of my adult life — at grassroots and national levels. Being a woman with privilege (particularly later in life) means that I can navigate this system with less difficulty (sometimes) than women without privilege; that is, by virtue of my race or class for example. I try to use my privilege to dismantle systems of inequality and level the playing field any way I can. Women experience different levels of privilege and oppression and that is something that requires organizing and social movements — to work in solidarity and collectively to take actions that go beyond inclusion. We need to challenge structures that maintain privilege and oppression both outside of the schools and potentially within the schools.

Feminist labour education can be a location for acknowledging difference and using an intersectional lens. For me, this has been especially highlighted in my work with the Canadian Research Institute for the Advancement of Women (CRIAW-ICREF). CRIAW is known for its work on intersectional feminist frameworks (IFFs).

> IFFs aim to foster understanding of the many circumstances that combine with discriminatory social practices to produce and sustain inequality and exclusion. IFFs look at how systems of discrimination, such as colonialism and globalization, can impact the combination of a person's social or economic status; race; class; gender; sexuality; geographic location, citizenship, ability and other factors. (CRIAW 2006: 6–7)

CRIAW acknowledges that intersections of identity are not just those we put upon ourselves; sometimes they are labels or identities that others inflict on us. Ideas around intersectionality are significant for the PSUW because, although there are scholarships to include women who typically cannot access union schools, the success of these efforts is not clear. It raises questions. For example, how many women of colour are on the PSUW Steering Committee? How is diversity understood and upheld in decision-making? How are women supported when they challenge issues of discrimination based on representations of difference? Can the PSUW become more clearly a model of intersectionality? Without doing this, what kind of feminism does it model?

WHAT DOES FEMINISM IN LABOUR EDUCATION MEAN?

Cindy: Feminism can be messy, difficult and rewarding. Ideally it involves collective decision-making and, hard as this is, it leaves a sense of empowerment and responsibility with those who participate. Feminism in labour education deals with issues of power, position or privilege, and of oppression. According to popular education mantras, the actions we take through education should be guided by praxis: the integration of theory and practice. Perhaps then theories of feminism, or of including feminism as a topic of study at the school, might be considered. This might also offer the PSUW participants an opportunity to discuss a concept that many find frightening at first.

Adriane: Feminism in labour education encompasses not just the topics chosen for courses and plenaries but the way in which courses are designed and facilitated *and* the way in which the entire education project is conceived of and organized from the beginning. It means involving as many women as possible in as many activities from the beginning, as messy as that might be. It means not only identifying and tackling gender-based barriers to participation but also barriers that women face on the basis of race, sexual orientation, ability, family status and so on. Having said that, I acknowledge that the founders of the PSUW did not explicitly discuss what we meant when we talked about feminist labour education. By assuming that we all understood what we meant by that concept, we missed the chance to notice gaps in our vision and any groups of women we were leaving out.

WHAT IS FEMINIST WITHIN THE PSUW?

Adriane: One collective behaviour or reflex should be examining power relations among ourselves. In most parts of the labour movement today, if a school or program resists bureaucratization and involves a constantly changing group of largely rank-and-file volunteers in planning, logistics and facilitation, then it will likely involve women with diverse class backgrounds (occupations, education and income levels) and probably women of different age groups. But other kinds of measures need to be taken to ensure a diversity of races, sexual orientations and abilities in our events. The PSUW has had mixed success in achieving this redistribution of power. While we offered courses like Union Women on Turtle Island; Women, Work and Ability; and Inside and Out, facilitated by Indigenous women, women with disabilities and lesbian women, respectively, we have not yet developed systems to ensure representative access by and involvement of diverse women in all school activities.

In terms of personal behaviours that challenge unequal power, long-term school facilitators and organizers can and should just say "no" as a way of opening-up opportunities for others, and by that, I mean not accepting that invitation to facilitate a course for the fifth year in a row. Instead, it is important to make space for someone else to facilitate. Maybe she would not facilitate as well as I did; she certainly would not facilitate in the same way, but sharing roles is a means for another woman to gain the experience I once had the chance to gain. Sharing is a means to insert different voices and views into the learning environment. Another way long-term facilitators could equalize power is to give notice that we will not facilitate again unless we are paired with a newer facilitator to whom we can pass the torch.

That is really hard to do, especially when you love the course or the school, or both. You might notice that I was on the PSUW Steering Committee for sixteen years. So clearly, I have challenges practising what I preach. I did make a point of refusing to facilitate the same course more than three times in a row. I had a difficult time breaking all connections with the school. As the other founders retired or moved on to other roles and I was "the last woman standing," I think I felt some responsibility to maintain continuity or a link with the past. And it was ego: I have something important to contribute! They need me! And it was fun. It was not until I took a job in another, non-prairie province that I finally let go of taking an active role. I am still there in spirit.

Cindy: Perhaps one of the most difficult things about a feminist practice is implementing reflexivity — that is, negotiating how power and position are shaping the dynamics of the research and learning. Essentially what Adriane just shared here is her own critical reflection on leaving the Steering Committee. Perhaps this explains power in operation. The power we are most familiar with is the power of a dominant knowledge or way of doing things that keep structures and ideas revolving in the same way. We also need to think about how the power is being resisted. These are important concepts to explore as they assist in understanding structural power in operation.

Reflexivity is not just about the individual questioning of ways that power is being orchestrated; it is also about group reflexivity — that is, how we are working and learning together? In the research projects I did with the PSUW between 2012 and 2015 there was a reciprocal relationship that was both supportive and challenging. Although I was always welcomed and accommodated, once decisions were made about next steps, the dialogue ended. I was left wondering whether it was really PAR — how and why was I excluded from the actions? I asked myself why I felt I should be part of the action. Taking a reflexive stance made me imagine what may have happened. I was not part of the school. It was a community-university relationship and I was still an outsider. The structures of power that are built into the community-based research processes are ever-present and within them friction always exists.

At the end of the first study, the Steering Committee decided that one of the key recommendations they wanted to implement was to keep a feminist focus. There was still not a clear definition of what that meant. I think it is time to revisit what feminism is within the school. Having this knowledge and using theories of feminism to guide them, might help shape future directions within the school and the understanding of how power operates within it.

IS THIS A LOVE LETTER JUST TO THE PSUW?

Cindy: As an academic living in Saskatchewan, my exposure to women's labour schools is limited. The two research studies we carried out with the PSUW offered me unique and exciting insights into what was happening at the school. Those insights have been shared widely as a result of the studies — through articles, a radio program, presentations and now the book. One paper presented received the Phyllis Cunningham Award for Social Justice (Hanson 2012), thus acknowledging that the PSUW was significant in the larger world of adult education for social justice. I hope that this chapter and this book encourage other labour educators to reflect and share the stories that emerge from their work. There is no doubt that as Kirton (2017) suggests, "strong unions need women" and a key ingredient in developing strong women is labour education that works to shatter the glass ceiling.

Adriane: At the time of writing, the Prairie School for Union Women is the longest-running women-only labour school in Canada. That's one reason. And it's the school I — and we — know best, in intimate detail, both from lived experience and from the research projects. While I know some things about other schools, especially from working on this book, I'm not in any position to comment on those events. That would be presumptuous.

After one of our first presentations about the PSUW research, a woman in the audience asked, "Are you saying that the Prairie School for Union Women is better than other women's schools?" No, we are not. For all that I love and admire the PSUW, it is important to resist putting it on a pedestal. The great things that happen at the PSUW can be replicated and improved upon elsewhere. We studied it and write about it to encourage more women's labour education. Here's to more imitation and innovation!

REFERENCES

Ballantyne, Morna. 2014. "Report to ETFO on Focus Groups on Women's Programs." Unpublished research report. Available in ETFO archives.

Boal, Augusto. 2000. *Theatre of the Oppressed.* London: Pluto Press.

Briskin, Linda. 2006. "Victimization and Agency: The Social Construction of Union Women's Leadership." Special Issue on Gender and Industrial Relations. *Industrial Relations Journal,* 37, 4.

____. 1999. "Union Leadership and Equity Representation. Paper for the Union Module of the Gender and Work Database." <genderwork.ca/gwd/wp-content/uploads/Briskin_Union-Leadership_Paper_April_2006.pdf>.

Briskin, Linda, Sue Genge, Margaret McPhail, and Marion Pollack. 2013. "Making Time for Equality." *Our Times* 32, 1.

Briskin, Linda, and Patricia McDermott. 1993. *Women Challenging Unions: Feminism, Democracy, and Militancy.* Toronto: University of Toronto Press.

Burke, Beverley, and Suzanne Doerge. 2000. *Starting with Women's Lives: Changing Today's Economy.* Second ed. OPSEU.

Burke, Bev, Jojo Geronimo, D'Arcy Martin, Barb Thomas, and Carol Wall. 2002. *Education for Changing Unions.* Toronto: Between the Lines.

Busman, G. 1981. "Case Studies: How to Develop and Use Them." In B.M. Wertheimer (ed.), *Labor Education for Working Women.* Philadelphia: Temple University Press.

Cambridge Documentary Films; directed and produced by Margaret Lazarus [and] Renner Wunderlich. 2001. *The Strength to Resist: Media's Impact on Women & Girls.* Cambridge, MA.

Carter, Sue, and D'Arcy Martin. 2013. "Equip, Engage, Expand, and Energize: Labour Movement Education." In Tom Nesbit, Susan M. Brigham, Nancy Taber, and Tara Gibb (eds.), *Building on Critical Traditions: Adult Education and Learning in Canada.* Toronto: Thompson Educational Publishing.

Catlett, Judith A. 1986. "After the Goodbyes: A Long-term Look at the Southern School for Women Workers." *Labor Studies Journal,* 10, 3 (Winter).

Central American Women's Network (CAWN). 2008. Resumen Informativo. *La Alfabetizacion Economica.* October. <cawn.org/assets/CAWN%20 Alfabetizacion%20Economica.pdf >.

Clark, Paul F. 2000. *Building More Effective Unions.* Ithaca, NY: Cornell University Press.

CRIAW (Canadian Research Institute for the Advancement of Women). 2006. *Intersectional Feminist Frameworks: A Primer.* Ottawa: CRIAW.

CUPE (Canadian Union of Public Employees). 2005. "Women Breaking Barriers 5-day Course Facilitator's Notes." Ottawa: CUPE Union Development Department.

____. 2007. "Strengthening our Union: Final Report of CUPE's National Women's Task Force." <cupe.ca/final-report-national-womens-task-force>.

____. 2014. "CUPE celebrates, Year in Review." <cupe.ca/sites/cupe/files/celebrate2014english_final.pdf>.

____. 2015. "CUPE Membership Survey Results for Equality." <cupe.ca/cupe-membership-survey-results-equality>.

Doerge, Suzanne, and Fernández Piñon. 2004. *Transformando la economía de hoy desde la vida cotidiana de las mujeres.* Steelworkers Humanity Fund. [Original English version by Beverley Burke and Suzanne Doerge.]

Elkiss, Helen. 1994. "Training Women for Union Office: Breaking the Glass Ceiling." *Labor Studies Journal*, 19, 2.

Elliot, Patricia W. 2011. *Participatory Action Research: Challenges, Complications and Opportunities*. Saskatoon: Centre for the Study of Cooperatives.

Enwright, Erin, Jack McGlinn, and Tom Juravich. 1996. "An Evaluation of the Women's Institute for Leadership Development." University of Massachusetts Amherst: Labor Relations and Research Center.

Eulo, R.M. 2015. Personal communication via email, May 7.

Fournier, Catherine. 2005. "Executive Summary: Leaders for Tomorrow Course Qualitative Assessment." Available at ETFO archives.

Freire, Paulo. 1970. *Pedagogy of the Oppressed*. New York: Continuum.

___. 1997. *Pedagogy of the Heart*. New York: Continuum.

___. 2000. *Pedagogy of the Oppressed*. New York: Continuum.

Greene, Anne-Marie, and Gill Kirton. 2002. "The Role of Women-Only Trade Union Education." *Gender, Work and Organization*, 9, 1.

Hall, Brad. "President's Report." 2007. *Union Expressed*, 1, 6 (Nov/Dec). <947.cupe. ca/updir/947/Nov_Dec_2007.pdf>.

Hanson, Cindy. 2012a. "Community-Based Participatory Research with the Prairie School for Union Women (Winner of Phyllis Cunningham Award for Social Justice)." Paper presentation at Proceedings of the 53rd Annual Adult Education Research Conference. June 2012, (pp. 146–54). Saratoga Springs, NY. <https:// newprairiepress.org/aerc/2012/papers/21/>.

___. 2012b. "Innovations, Opportunities, and Challenges: The Story of the Prairie School for Union Women." Unpublished research report, March 8. <sfl.sk.ca/ public/images/documents/Events/Annual%20Schools/PSUW_Report_-_ March-2012.pdf>.

___. 2015. "'I Learned I Am a Feminist': Lessons for Adult Learning from Participatory Action Research with Union Women." *Canadian Journal for the Study of Adult Education*, 27, 1.

Hesser, Terry Spencer. 2008. *I Am a Teamster: A Short, Fiery Story of Regina V. Polk, Her Hats, Her Pets, Sweet Love, and the Modern-Day Labor Movement*. Chicago: Lake Claremont Press.

hooks, bell. 2003. *Teaching Community. A Pedagogy of Hope*. New York: Routledge.

Kagis, Aina, and Barb Byers. 2017. "Our Past Is Prologue." *Briarpatch*, October 23 (November/December). <briarpatchmagazine.com/articles/view/our-past-is-prologue>

Kainer, Jan. 2006. "Gendering Union Renewal: Women's Contributions to Labour Movement Revitalization." <libgwd.cns.yorku.ca/gwd/wp-content/uploads/ Kainer_Gendering_Union_Renewal.pdf>.

KAIROS: Canadian Ecumenical Justice Initiatives. 1997, revised 2016. "The Blanket Exercise." Toronto, ON.

Kirton, Gill. 2017. "From 'A Woman's Place Is in her Union' to 'Strong Unions Need Women': Changing Gender Discourses, Policies and Realities in the Union Movement." *Labour & Industry: A Journal of the Social and Economic Relations of Work*, 27, 4.

Kirton, Gill, and Geraldine Healy. 2004. "Shaping Union and Gender Identities: A Case Study of Women-Only Trade Union Courses." *British Journal of Industrial*

Relations, 42, 2.

Landsberg, Michelle. 2011. *Writing the Revolution.* Toronto: Second Story Press.

Manicom, Linzi, and Shirley Walters (eds.). 2012. *Feminist Popular Education in Transnational Debates: Building Pedagogies of Possibility.* New York: Palgrave Macmillan.

McGough, Jim. 1996–2005. "Stier Anderson & Malone Reports on Organized Crime Influence in Teamster Union, Lack of 'Good Faith' by Hoffa in Reforming Teamsters, and Corruption in Chicago." Laborers for JUSTICE. <ipsn.org/stier_anderson_malone_reports.htm>.

Melcher, Dale, Jennifer L. Eichstedt, Shelley Eriksen, and Dan Clawson. 1992. "Women's Participation in Local Union Leadership: The Massachusetts Experience." *Industrial and Labor Relations Review,* 45, 2.

Paavo, Adriane. 2006. "Union Workload: A Barrier to Women Surviving Labour-Movement Leadership." *Just Labour* 8.

___. 2001. "The Prairie School for Union Women: An Intuitive Promoter of Lifelong Learning." Unpublished research paper. Course requirement for master's at Ontario Institute for Studies in Eduation, University of Toronto.

Public Service International. 2002. "Wall Display Guide." Unpublished participant manual. PSI Congress: Ottawa (Sept. 2–6).

Raposo, Lesley, Carrie Robinson, Marie Kelly, and Kathleen Grant. 2003. "Strong Women, Strong Union: Women and Organizing." *Our Times,* 22, 3.

Ross, Stephanie, Larry Savage, Errol Black, and Jim Silver. 2015. *Building a Better World: An Introduction to the Labour Movement in Canada,* 3rd edition. Halifax: Fernwood Publishing.

Schwartz, Kristin. 2009. "Leaders for Tomorrow." *Our Times,* 28, 1.

Shaughnessy, Kate, and Gayle Hamilton. 2015. "Union Women's Leadership Education Project: Report Summary." March. Orlando, FL: UALE Orlando Conference.

Spagnuolo, Mario, and Larry A. Glassford. 2008. "Feminism in Transition: The Margaret Tomen Membership Case and the Formation of the Elementary Teachers Federation of Ontario." *Historical Studies in Education/Revue d'histoire de l'éducation,* Fall.

Starhawk. 1989. "The Three Types of Power." *Truth or Dare: Encounters with Power, Authority and Mystery.* San Francisco: Harpers.

Twarog, Emily. 2016. "The Polk School: Intersections of Women's Labor Leadership Education and the Public Sphere." In Dennis Deslippe, Eric Fore-Slocum, and John McKerley (eds.), *Civic Labors: Scholars, Teachers, Activists, and Working-Class History.* Urbana: University of Illinois Press.

Twarog, Emily E. LB., Jennifer Sherer, Brigid O'Farrell, and Cheryl Coney. 2016. "Labor Education and Leadership Development for Union Women: Assessing the Past, Building for the Future." *Labor Studies Journal* 41, 1.

Walters, Shirley, and Linzi Manicom (eds.). 1996. *Gender in Popular Education: Methods for Empowerment.* London: Zed Books.

Worthen, Helena, Michelle Kaminski, and Jocelyn Graf. 2005. "Women's Labor Education: Impact and Insights." Unpublished research report. Previous title: Kaminski, Michelle, Helena Worthen, and Jocelyn Graf. 2002. "Ten Years of Union Women's Leadership Training: Impact of Union Commitment and Participation." Available from the author.

CONTRIBUTORS

We acknowledge the Sisters in Labour Education, who came together to contribute to this book about women-only labour schools and programs.

SANDRA AHENEKEW works for the Indigenous Services Canada and is a member of the Public Service Alliance of Canada. She is from Treaty Six, Ahtahkakoop First Nation and lives in Regina, Saskatchewan. She co-facilitated Union Women on Turtle Island with Yvonne Hotzak.

MORNA BALLANTYNE signed her first union card in 1977. During her thirty years with the Canadian Union of Public Employees, she served in many senior staff positions, including director of union development. Women Breaking Barriers was one of several new and innovative education initiatives that she and the education team introduced to increase capacity for class analysis and to train activists to lead progressive change.

BARBARA M. BYERS was president of the Saskatchewan Federation of Labour from 1988–2002. She served as one of the Canadian Labour Congress's executive vice-presidents beginning in 2002 and then its secretary-treasurer from 2014–17. In 2015 she was named a member of the Order of Canada.

BEV BURKE is an adult educator who has worked with community groups, unions, women's organizations and international non-government organizations both in Canada and internationally, primarily in Latin America and Africa. Most of her recent work has been with labour unions.

SUZANNE DOERGE has built on her experience as a health educator in Nicaragua to facilitate workshops on equity and social justice. For ten years, she has served as director for the City for All Women initiative in Ottawa, which seeks to advance gender equality and promote a more inclusive city.

TESS EWING has been a labour activist since the 1970s, when she was one of the organizers of the Boston School Bus Drivers Union. While labour extension coordinator at University of Massachusetts Boston, she was an officer of the UMass professional staff union, PSU/MTA. Now retired, she continues her activism in the Women's Institute for Leadership Development.

CINDY HANSON teaches adult education at the University of Regina and from 2016–2018 served as the president of the Canadian Research Institute for the Advancement of Women (CRIAW-ICREF), a national, feminist research organization in Canada. Her research uses participatory and intersectional approaches, often with communities engaged in non-formal, feminist, Indigenous and/or intergenerational learning. She has conducted research with the PSUW and the Labour College of Canada. One of Cindy's publications about the PSUW received the Phyllis Cunningham Award for Social Justice (Hanson 2012a).

YVONNE HOTZAK is Cree from Cowessess First Nation in Saskatchewan. She is president of the board of directors of the Museum Association of Saskatchewan. Yvonne has been a registered nurse for thirty-three years. She co-facilitated a course called Union Women on Turtle Island with Sandra Ahenekew.

DALE MELCHER is a labour educator, a former extension coordinator at the University of Massachusetts Amherst and a member of the Massachusetts Teachers Association. She has been involved with both the Women's Institute for Leadership Development and the UALE Northeast Summer School for Union Women. Her work focuses on women and work and leadership development.

ADRIANE PAAVO is one of the founders of the Prairie School for Union Women and remained actively involved until 2013. She fell in love with labour education while working as a staff representative with the Grain Services Union. She has since worked in the education departments of other private- and public-sector unions in Canada. Her master's thesis is entitled "Eight Days a Week: How Union Workload Blocks Women's Leadership in the Union Movement."

DONNA SMITH works at the Saskatchewan Federation of Labour. She sits on the SFL and Canadian Labour Congress's Solidarity and Pride Committee and has been on the CUPE National Pink Triangle Committee as the Saskatchewan representative for several years. She is an advocate, lobbyist and educator on LGBTQ issues.

JANE STINSON worked at the Canadian Union of Public Employees national office doing research, member education, staff training and national union initiatives (1980–2009). She also is active in the Canadian Research Institute for the Advancement of Women/Institut canadien de recherches sur les femmes (CRIAW/ICREF), on the board of directors (2004–09), leading the Feminist Northern Network for CRIAW (2010–16) and investigating the impacts of changing public services on diverse women as workers and users of those services (2012–17).

BARB THOMAS is an educator, writer, facilitator and organizational developer committed to promoting equity and democratic process in organizations. She has worked with unions and other non-profit organizations in Canada and internationally, including Toronto's Cross Cultural Communication Centre, the Doris Marshall Institute for Education and Action, the Ontario Human Rights Commission, Service Employees International Union in Canada and the Ontario Public Service Employees Union. She is a co-author of, among other publications, *Educating for a Change*; *Education for Changing Unions*; and *Dancing on Live Embers: Challenging Racism in Organizations*.

SUSAN WINNING has been the director of the Labor Education Program at the University of Massachusetts, Lowell for almost fifteen years, providing education, training and organizational support for unions, labour councils and community organizations. Prior to that, she worked as the executive director of the Women's Institute for Leadership Development.

HELENA WORTHEN retired from the University of Illinois Labor Education Program in 2010 and moved, with her husband Joe Berry, to Berkeley, California, near her children and grandchildren. In 2015–16 she taught in the Labour Relations and Trade Unions Faculty at Ton Duc Thang University in Ho Chi Minh City, Vietnam. She is the author of the prize-winning book *What Did You Learn at Work Today?* from Hardball Press. Her academic field is learning theory in the socio-cultural tradition, taking the workplace as a contested site of the creation of power through learning.

CAROL ZAVITZ works at the Elementary Teachers' Federation of Ontario and was involved in developing and running Leaders for Tomorrow (L4T) for its first six years.